MW01015218

Motivation Matters

A Workbook for

School Change

Margery B. Ginsberg

with Pablo Fiene

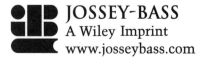

JOSSEY-BASS
A Wiley Imprint
www.josseybass.com

Published by Jossey-Bass
A Wiley Imprint
989 Market Street, San Francisco, CA 94103-1741   www.josseybass.com

Jossey-Bass books and products are available through most bookstores. To contact Jossey-Bass directly call our Customer Care Department within the U.S. at 800-956-7739, outside the U.S. at 317-572-3986 or fax 317-572-4002.

Jossey-Bass also publishes its books in a variety of electronic formats. Some content that appears in print may not be available in electronic books.

ISBN 0-7879-6471-9

Printed in the United States of America

FIRST EDITION

PB Printing   10 9 8 7 6 5 4 3 2 1

A joint publication in
The Jossey-Bass Education Series
and
The Jossey-Bass Higher
and Adult Education Series

Contents

Acknowledgments

A manual such as this is based on the work of educators who apply ideas with such skill that my own work is transformed. For their expertise and support, I convey my heartfelt appreciation to friends, colleagues, and students at Spring Woods High School and Spring Oaks Middle School in Houston, Texas, and to Horace Cureton Elementary School, Lester Shields Elementary School, and Joseph George Middle School in San Jose, California. Public schools have been the primary laboratories for the strategies in this text. Amidst the erosion of public confidence and funding, transitions in school leadership and staff, and changes in curriculum, most of the people with whom I have worked meet the daily challenge of helping each student reach inside themselves for their many gifts.

I would also like to thank Gale Erlandson who is no longer an editor at Jossey-Bass and David Brightman and Leslie Iura, who are. These editors are fundamentally respectful of and responsive to authors. This is also true of Cathy Mallon who oversaw, and Genevieve Duboscq who performed, the copyediting for this book. As well, I convey my gratitude to Jessica Egbert, for her "right-there" marketing assistance.

There are those who follow my progress and work on a daily basis. Raymond Wlodkowski is my husband. Suzanne Benally, Charles Naumer, and Sonny Zinn are my friends. I thank them for respecting my doubts about the enormous moral responsibility I feel for introducing changes when there are so many pressures on the lives and work of educators.

I would also like to thank colleagues and friends who opened doors because they believe in this work. They include Barbara Noorgard-Reid, Lois LaShell, Lorenzo Garcia, Norma Martinez, Debbie Tito, Sylvia Campbell, Pablo Fiene, Anita Villarreal, Amy Anderson, Cindy Harrison, Jan Herrera, Patricia Schaffarczyk, Michelle Karns, Wendy Hurst, and Teresa Lopez.

My children, Matthew Aaron and Daniel Mark, are the impetus for all of my work. They remind me that you can't seek change unless you are willing to try to live it yourself. As students, they appreciate the need for theory building as well as artful teaching.

My parents, Kit and Aubrey Ettenheimer, are always supportive, even though they don't think I put enough humor in my writing. My Aunt Marianne Rubiner, a maverick woman and former teacher, has paid attention to my ideas and to my heart for a very long time. Let me just say "thank you."

Margery B. Ginsberg
June 2003

About the Author

With a background as a teacher on two Indian reservations, a university professor, and a Texas Title I technical assistance contact for the United States Department of Education, Margery Ginsberg is an independent researcher and consultant in Boulder, Colorado. She works nationally and internationally to provide support for comprehensive school renewal anchored in a culturally responsive and motivationally significant pedagogy. Her work has been the foundation for several comprehensive school reform demonstration designs, including one of two high schools to receive the 1999–2000 United States Department of Education Model National Professional Development Award.

In addition to *Motivation Matters: A Workbook for School Change* (Jossey-Bass, 2003), Dr. Ginsberg's books are *Creating Highly Motivating Classrooms for All Students: A Schoolwide Approach to Powerful Teaching with Diverse Learners* (Jossey-Bass, 2000), *Educators Supporting Educators: A Guide to Organizing School Support Teams* (Association for Supervision and Curriculum Development, 1997), and *Diversity and Motivation: Culturally Responsive Teaching* (with Raymond Wlodkowski, Jossey-Bass, 1995). Dr. Ginsberg's work provided the foundational material for two video series, *Motivation: The Key to Teaching and Learning* (Association for Supervision and Curriculum Development, 2003) and *Encouraging Motivation Among All Students* (Video Journal of Education, 1996). She has a Ph.D. in bilingual/multicultural/social foundations of education from the University of Colorado-Boulder.

Introduction

THIS BOOK PROVIDES concrete approaches to facilitate school renewal based on principles of intrinsic motivation—among students and educators. It describes strategies that award-winning high-poverty public schools have used to become not only more inclusive of but more relevant and challenging to students of diverse student groups. In these schools academic achievement has increased; disproportional rates of achievement among diverse student groups is being reduced; and incidents of school violence have sharply declined.

Although many factors influence the success of ongoing school renewal, in all of the schools that have tested the strategies in this book, teachers regularly work together to share their expertise and engage in inquiry. The approaches these teachers use vary according to the unique strengths, challenges, and aspirations of the school, but all these teachers have one thing in common: they focus on the before, during, and after of lesson or unit design by planning learning experiences together, opening their classroom doors to one another, and engaging in reflective practices through action research, lesson study, and the examination of student work.

Instructional practice and its influence on student motivation and learning is the central concern of successful schools. All other school improvement considerations complement this emphasis. Governance structures, scheduling, family and community involvement, environment, safety, and counseling are important to the extent that they help a school develop its focus on curriculum, instruction, and assessment. As Richard Elmore (2002, p. 1) explains, "We are viscerally and instinctively inclined to move the boxes around on the organizational chart, to fiddle with the schedule. We are attracted and drawn to these things largely because they're visible and, believe it or not, easier to do than to make the hard changes, which are in instructional practice." The academic community is in general agreement that public schools in the United States that sustain the centrality of school-wide instructional practice are seeing impressive gains in student performance (Elmore, 2002; Neumann, 1999; Noguera and Moran Brown, 2002). A requisite to accomplishing this is a coherent professional development plan that serves as the cornerstone of school improvement—whether school improvement is based on a schoolwide plan in which funding streams are coordinated, a comprehensive school reform demonstration grant, a state-mandated change process, or a district template for annual and ongoing improvement.

Typically, the professional development plans of successful schools are the creation of teachers and school-based administrators, with support from a district representative or an external facilitator. Adult learning is embedded in the same motivational conditions that teachers aspire to create in their classrooms for students. The pedagogical language to maintain this focus on *intrinsically motivating pedagogy*—instructional practice that encourages learning because the learning itself is of value—may vary from the conceptual framework presented in this book. But whatever the language they use, successful schools seek schoolwide agreement on this: all students of all backgrounds are entitled to and thrive on learning that is emotionally, socially, and cognitively significant and rewarding. This is the essence of intrinsic motivation. The tools in this book have been created and field-tested with instructionally focused, motivationally anchored school improvement in mind.

Although intrinsic motivation can work in partnership with extrinsic rewards, for example, national awards and recognition, if learning is to be cognitively significant, it must be compelling (Deci and Ryan, 1991; Lambert and McCombs, 1998). Many educators, of course, agree that finding ways to encourage intrinsic motivation among students is essential, but the challenge can be daunting. In classrooms as diverse as those within the United States, motivation is inseparable from the historical, political, and contemporary influences on students and families. Student motivation, educational equity, and academic achievement require an understanding of how students learn as individuals and as members of their communities (Cohen, McLaughlin, and Talbert, 1993; Darling-Hammond and McLaughlin, 1995; McCombs, 1999). Teaching also requires a willingness to grapple with hard questions concerning race, racism, and our personal responsibility as educators. These issues have not historically been a significant part of the teacher education programs.

This is a primary reason that professional development is the linchpin of school reform aimed at raising academic performance. No amount of standards, benchmarks, and high-stakes testing can bring about school improvement without attention to teachers' knowledge and practices, grounded within the context of the communities they serve (Ladson-Billings and Gomez, 2001). Based on traditions of success in U.S. schools, especially in high-poverty public schools, all of the renewal strategies in this book are within the teacher's sphere of influence and can become a part of daily professional development—although sometimes not without conflict. Because school change is controversial, several of the tools include ways to access ideas and methods that can help teachers cross boundaries that interfere with teacher collaboration and continuous improvement.

This book is a resource guide that stands alone. But it is most informative when used in conjunction with two other texts on motivationally anchored kindergarten through postsecondary renewal. *Creating Highly Motivating Classrooms for All Students: A Schoolwide Approach to Powerful Teaching with Diverse Learners* (Ginsberg and Wlodkowski, 2000) and *Diversity and Motivation: Culturally Responsive Teaching* (Wlodkowski and Ginsberg, 1995) provide a thorough examination of the cultural and theoretical foundations of the strategies within this text.

Five Themes for Successful School Renewal

This book categorizes strategies under five themes, each a significant influence on successful school renewal:

- Using a schoolwide motivationally anchored language for teaching and learning
- Facilitating collaborative adult learning
- Using data in ways that go beyond high-stakes tests
- Aligning advocacy for school change and support
- Creating a signature or identity that goes beyond conventional vision statements

Chapter One provides background on the role of intrinsic motivation in school renewal and introduces a pedagogical language that Raymond Wlodkowski and I (Ginsberg and Wlodkowski, 2000) call the motivational framework for culturally responsive teaching. I encourage the schools with which I work to examine, apply, use, and elaborate on this framework to capture and share teacher knowledge. We created the motivational framework in 1995, but it has been made significant by teachers in schools throughout the United States, Europe, and Asia who have taken these principles to heart and used them to create high-performing schools where

students and staff alike possess the will and the skill to engage in courageous learning. The first chapter also introduces the importance of a schoolwide instructional leadership cadre, a team of change advocates who work
for school-based professional development. Chapter One includes case
studies that integrate and illustrate several strategies to advance the success of a school.

Chapter Two introduces the instructional leadership cadre, whose members are the core of this kind of school renewal initiative. They are the first
members of the school community to learn the language of the motivational
framework, personalize its potential, apply it to their practice, and cocreate
ways to introduce it to the school community as a whole. The chapter
includes several strategies for selecting, organizing, developing, and focusing a cadre. It also includes forms for meetings and forms for the school-
based reform coach, if a school is fortunate enough to have such a person.
In addition, Chapter Two contains a professional development organizer
that can help the school community ensure that its various goals and
processes complement one another.

Chapter Three is about schoolwide collaboration. It provides ideas for
finding additional time, helping grade-level or content teams focus their
planning on motivating instruction and ways to assess student learning. It
also provides efficient approaches to peer coaching, analysis of lessons
through lesson studies, and collective problem solving. As with all of the
chapters, Chapter Three provides several useful forms to guide processes.
These are easy to duplicate and customize.

Chapter Four provides approaches to two kinds of data: (1) original data
related to student motivation and learning and professional development
benchmarks and (2) data from standardized tests. Two of the most popular
forms of collecting original data are five-minute walk-throughs and data in
a day. The walk-through helps administrators to strengthen their role as
instructional leaders. At the same time, these help principals gather data to
provide regular and comprehensive feedback to the school community on
the extent to which teachers are anchoring practice in principles of motivation. Data in a day is another example of a process that schools value. It is
a collaborative action-research approach that includes parents, community
members, teachers, and, when appropriate, students who visit classrooms
to take "snapshots" of how teaching looks throughout an entire school in a
single day. This chapter also provides sample schoolwide plans and benchmarks for accomplishing professional development and other goals. Further, it provides an approach to creating a school portfolio that illustrates
the school community, provides a communication tool for its members, and
allows a school community to reflect on its accomplishments.

The focus of Chapter Five is signature and advocacy. *Signature* is a theme that excites a school community and integrates academic goals. Schools ask themselves: What do we want to model for the nation as a visionary demonstration site? Examples include community learning, literacy across the curriculum, technology and publishing, or as illustrated in Exhibit 5.2, integrating arts and literacy. *Advocacy* refers to the essential role of students, families, community members, and district personnel in rallying support for innovation. This chapter provides case studies that illustrate how schools can define a signature that helps everyone to pull in the same direction.

Chapter 1

Using a Motivationally Anchored Language for Teaching and Learning

MOTIVATION IS the answer to the difficult question: Why do we do what we do? In education conceptions of wisdom as well as research indicate that motivated students will surpass unmotivated students in learning and performance. Therefore, it stands to reason that knowledge about motivation can support academic achievement among a broad range of students. But knowledge about motivation also serves as a guide for the learning and organizational needs of adults engaged in school renewal. This is especially relevant at a time when the teaching profession is undergoing enormous pressure for enhanced accountability and teachers are tempted to take the most cursory approach to accomplish externally imposed mandates. For some time many educators have felt as if they are being asked to redress problems for which all of society ought to bear responsibility. Undoubtedly, the scarcity of resources devoted to public education only exacerbates teachers' frustration. Nonetheless, legitimate concerns about fiscal and human limitations and political agendas can mask the inspiring accomplishments of public schools, many among them in communities of the highest poverty. According to scholars such as Asa Hilliard, it is the will to change how we teach that has been missing (Lewis, 2001).

A key assumption of this book is that in order for educators to strengthen their will and their skill to make the changes necessary to support the learning of a broader range of students, especially historically underserved students, communities must provide both pressure and support (Fullan and Miles, 1992). Support includes not only time and fiscal resources but methods of collaboration built upon key conditions for motivation. These conditions include respect, choices that have relevance and meaning, and evidence of success that matters to learners.

This does not diminish the need for leaders at all levels of responsibility to demonstrate a sustained, enthusiastic commitment to a visionary direction. Leaders must have the courage to safeguard against disconnected and fragmented school-improvement efforts that undermine meaningful change. Far too often, when implementing new ideas brings on the inevitable messiness, teachers and administrators quit and search anew for a quick and easy answer (DuFour, 2002). Nothing is more destructive to the cause of school change than the tendency of schools to move by fits and starts, to reverse direction, to behave in generally erratic ways (Schlechty, 2001). The fact that teachers have been able to bail out at times of adversity or wait for new ideas to pass with predictable changes in school boards and staff makes grounding adult learning in principles of intrinsic motivation especially necessary.

Motivation Resides in Everyone

Motivation is complex. When we teach we see that the same student who responded apathetically to a lecture may nonetheless energetically interact with peers on any number of topics in the hallway after class. Similarly, it is not uncommon for a student who is bored or frustrated in one class to actively participate in another. Realities of this sort help us to know that people are motivated by something even when they are not motivated to do what others would like them to do in the way that others would like them to do it. It is part of human nature to be curious, to be active, to initiate thought and behavior, to make meaning from experience, and to be effective at what we value (Lambert and McCombs, 1998). These primary sources of motivation reside in all of us, across all ethnic and cultural groups. When people can see that what they are learning makes sense and is important according to their values and perspectives, their motivation generally emerges. Like a cork rising through water, intrinsic motivation surfaces in a supportive environment (Ginsberg and Wlodkowski, 2000).

This is one of the reasons that schools and classrooms—and primary influences on schools and classrooms that support learning across various student groups—respect the role of race, ethnicity, and culture in motivation. Just from the perspective of emotions (as opposed to a more complex analysis of political and economic influences on motivation), we are socialized through culture. One person working at a task feels joy and continues. Another person feels frustrated or angry and does not persevere. And yet another person feels frustrated but continues with increased determination. Even though people within a group vary, emotions are socialized through culture. What elicits joy, frustration, or determination may differ across ethnic and cultural groups because of differences in historical and contemporary experiences, opportunities, perceptions, and ideas about accepted and appropriate responses to experiences. To a large extent, the response that a person has to a learning activity reflects his or her ethnic or cultural background (Kitayama and Markus, 1994; Gay, 2000).

From this viewpoint effectively teaching all students requires awareness and respect for cultural diversity, appreciation that all students are motivated, and determination to find ways to encourage that motivation. Although the internal logic as to why students do something may not coincide with that of the teacher, it is nonetheless present. To be consistently effective, the teacher has to understand that perspective. This can be particularly challenging because teachers too are influenced by their cultural experiences and philosophies. A common example of this, in a profession where only 13 percent of teachers are people of color, is European-American educators who have not, for whatever reasons, examined issues related to privilege and who maintain unquestioned assumptions about such things as effort and reward as a driving force in student learning. Learning is the act of making meaning from experience, and supporting the motivation of all students in learning requires designing instruction accordingly. What might this mean in terms of everyday lesson design?

Instructional Plans as Motivational Plans

For schools, especially those actively engaged in comprehensive school reform, this means that every instructional plan ought to be a motivational plan. But this can be a challenge. Finding an instructional design format for most subject matter is not difficult (Rothwell and Kazanas, 1992). However, most designs do not adequately deal with ethnic and cultural diversity. In many schools teachers try to do this independently, relying on intuition and spontaneous decision making, much of which is limited by a teacher's experiences and beliefs. Difficulties are most apparent when students' motivation seems low or diminishing. Without an adequate guide for planning and ways to revise, refine, or build upon a planned learning experience, teachers across racial, ethnic, and linguistic groups often feel helpless, hopeless, and prone to blame students for the difficulties. When they turn to books on motivation, the vast range of competing theories can confuse them further. When they turn to books about ethnic and cultural diversity, many are specific to certain groups. Although such books can yield valuable clues to teaching more effectively, the challenge is to think broadly while simultaneously respecting the unique bonds of specific groups and the unique attributes of individuals. This is important because if teachers fail to acknowledge the variation within ethnic and cultural groups, influenced by such factors as social class, gender, family narratives about and personal interpretations of historical and contemporary political conditions, they risk stereotyping or narrowly bracketing students according to prescribed lists of characteristics (Hilliard, 1989; Irvine and York, 1995).

Teachers need plans for fostering motivation that are flexible and that help them respond coherently to the complexities of human diversity. Without a plan, teaching too often becomes a process of trial and error, lacking cohesion and continuity. A plan gives all students a greater opportunity to experience academic success. Most importantly, perhaps, a shared conceptual framework for teaching and learning provides a context, a common language for adults to exchange ideas and provide focused collegial support to one another. But with so many theories on motivation, education, and school renewal, how might a cohesive conceptual design for pedagogy (and school renewal) look? How can we cohesively support human motivation—the natural human capacity to direct energy in pursuit of a goal—to make schools increasingly effective?

An Ecology Underlies Motivational Planning

First, we must recognize that motivation is a vital construct within the realm of many disciplines. These include philosophy, sociology, the study of spiritual ideology, economics, linguistics, anthropology, political science, and a host of other disciplines, including the field of education. In education alone the number of theories that inform the way we think about student motivation and learning contribute to an expansive knowledge base that includes multiple intelligences, language acquisition, brain-based learning, constructivism, cooperative learning, literacy theories, multicultural education, performance assessment, student-centered learning, and experiential learning.

What has been missing is an ecology with which to synthesize the concepts from the various disciplines that contribute to a comprehensive understanding of how to construct an environment that enhances motivation and learning for all students. Intrinsic motivation provides that synthesis, and it is the foundational theory for an approach to instructional planning that Raymond Wlodkowski and I (2000) call the motivational framework for culturally responsive teaching (although we encourage schools to rethink the language that we have chosen as labels in order to personalize the framework and make the principles they agree on accessible to everyone in the school community).

The Motivational Framework
for Culturally Responsive Teaching

The motivational framework for culturally responsive teaching (or simply the motivational framework) provides a *macrocultural* pedagogical model. It is built upon principles and structures that are meaningful within and across cultures, especially with students from families that have not historically experienced success in school systems. It does not compare and contrast groups of people from a microcultural perspective, one that, for example, identifies a specific ethnic group and prescribes approaches to teaching according to that group's presumed characteristics and orientations.

The purpose of the motivational framework is to unify teaching practices that elicit the intrinsic motivation of all learners so that educators can consistently design learning experiences that matter to and support the success of all students. Therefore, we have sought to make the framework broad enough that it accommodates the range of ethnic and cultural diversity found in most schools. It also integrates the variety of assumptions addressed in many disciplines—educational, political, social, and psychological. In terms of everyday instruction, it seeks to explain how to create compelling and democratic learning experiences that honor the diverse perspectives, values, and talents that students bring to the classroom.

Four Conditions of the Motivational Framework

The motivational framework (Exhibit 1.1, p. 28) offers a holistic representation of four basic conditions, or attributes in a learning environment, that work together to support a natural interest in learning:

- Establishing inclusion
- Developing a positive attitude
- Enhancing meaning
- Engendering competence

Establishing inclusion refers to principles and practices that contribute to a learning environment in which students and teachers feel respected by and connected to one another. Inclusion is the core of genuine empowerment and agency. As human beings, we seldom accept high levels of personal challenge unless we have a sense of emotional safety. If a student is to grapple with uncertainty and dissent, the learning environment must welcome the worth and expression of each person's true self. For this to occur, norms, procedures, and structures must contribute a sense of support and unity. Examples of this include communication agreements or ground rules (Chapter Two) and collaborative learning that promotes genuine opportunity for all people to contribute.

Developing a positive attitude refers to principles and practices that contribute, through personal and cultural relevance and through choice, to a favorable disposition toward learning. This means that learning is contextualized within the student's experience and is accessible to the student. It also means that students are encouraged to make real choices based on their experiences, values, strengths, and needs. It has been said that, generally, jurors make up their minds within the first ten minutes of a trial, after which influencing their opinions is most difficult. Students are in a parallel situation. Who among us will feel positively about learning when information and ways of defining talent exclude our own experiences and strengths? Examples of this motivational condition include personalized goal setting and approaches to accessing prior knowledge such as the KWL process where the teacher asks the students: What do you *know* about this topic? (K); *What* do you want to know? (W); and What have we *learned*? (L) (Ogle, 1986).

Enhancing meaning refers to challenging and engaging learning. It expands and strengthens learning in ways that matter to students and builds their identities as valued civic participants. Enhancing meaning is the condition that focuses on substantive learning experiences. This motivational condition is intellectually rigorous in ways that involve higher-order thinking and critical inquiry. Examples of this motivational condition are inquiry-oriented projects, role playing, problem solving, and case-study analysis.

Engendering competence refers to principles and practices that help students authentically identify what they know and can do and that give students a sense of hope. This motivational condition includes rubrics, tools that provide gradations of quality for each criterion of a successful paper, presentation, or product. Ideally, teachers create rubrics with students to clarify what success looks like. In addition to the rubrics, engendering competence also includes demonstrations of learning connected to students' frames of reference, self-assessment, and grading practices that encourage learning.

The four conditions work in concert to encourage and support the intrinsic motivation of a broad range of students, within and across cultural groups. Intrinsic motivation supports higher levels of cognition as well as the notion of lifelong learning (Deci and Ryan, 1985; Wlodkowski and Ginsberg, 1995; McCombs and Whistler, 1997). Unfortunately, many schools, and especially those that serve low-income populations, tend to rely strongly on extrinsic rewards. They commonly reward or punish students for behavior related to learning that lacks relevance, challenge, and success that matters. Strong schools know that no single teaching strategy will consistently engage all learners, but they also recognize that a repertoire of random strategies can be equally ineffective.

Pedagogical randomness can create motivational contradictions such as either cooperative learning combined with competitive assessment or project-based learning without the emotional safety for risk taking and inventiveness. Although some students are prepared to endure school under just about any circumstances, an increasing number of students are not. This is especially true of students who are neither implicitly nor explicitly connected to a hopeful future. For them school achievement does not promise impressive credentials, jobs, and incomes (Fordham and Ogbu, 1986).

Not only does the motivational framework include new teaching strategies for each condition, it also serves as a template for recognizing existing strengths in educational practice and providing clues to develop those strengths. In this way it is respectful of the work that educators are already doing while it encourages classroom teachers to apply principles of motivation for all students with constancy. To implement the motivational framework, readers will find sample lessons, units, and professional development sessions, as well as guidelines for faculty meetings, in Chapter Two.

As an adult educator who regularly provides demonstration classes to help teachers experience and encourage the courageous questioning of their practice, I know that "getting it right" is nearly impossible. In fact, one of the beautiful things about our profession is that we work with human beings, none of whom can be reduced to a checklist of pedagogical terms. But when used respectfully, a cohesive framework with which to identify strengths and generate clues for more motivationally effective teaching can contribute to a level of personal responsibility among educators that is optimistic and informative. In classrooms where educators are using the framework, we have seen exciting results.

A Low-Income Elementary School Uses the Motivational Framework to Guide School Renewal

A great deal of emphasis has been placed on the need for schools to carefully examine student achievement and other school data to create a well-informed approach to continuous school improvement. For many schools, however, this is the easy part. The real challenge is to link findings from such inquiry to decision making and professional development to which faculty will commit. That it why Henry Louis Elementary School, a composite of several courageous schools, is informative.

Henry Louis Elementary School

In the brief time Henry Louis Elementary School has been applying and evolving a comprehensive school-reform demonstration model focused on creating classrooms that are highly motivating for all students, their academic performance, as measured by state tests and teacher-designed assessments, has consistently increased. Although the educators at Henry Louis believe that test scores are a product of many influences, their ownership of the design and implementation of a motivationally grounded approach to teaching, professional development, and schoolwide reform are informative. Here is what Henry Louis is doing.

Henry Louis has an instructionally focused team of teachers, parents, and administrators. This team is called the renewal team, and team members refer to the four conditions of the motivational framework as IMACs, a mnemonic device: I stands for inclusion; M for meaning; A for attitude; and C for competence. Down the road a sister school refers to the motivational framework with the abbreviation IAMC, for "I am competent." The Henry Louis renewal team is modeling and guiding job-embedded professional development, and team members work with a district liaison and an external evaluator so that, amid the urgencies that occur on any given day, they have support for implementing their commitments.

As site-based professional developers and as teacher-researchers, they meet monthly, either independently or with an external consultant, to prepare to lead faculty meetings, collaboratively design lessons with their grade-level teams, videotape themselves for reflective lesson studies with colleagues, provide demonstration lessons in their classrooms, coach new teachers, and engage in collaborative action research to enhance the school's insight into the extent to which instructional practice is becoming more motivationally effective. They also meet weekly to follow through with plans from their monthly work sessions. An advocacy-oriented district liaison also attends these meetings.

The renewal team's leadership is anchored in research on how to support the intrinsic motivation of a broad range of students, as represented in a guiding resource, *Creating Highly Motivating Classrooms for All Students* (Ginsberg and Wlodkowski, 2000). Although Henry Louis's external consultant is a coauthor of the book, the school's approach is not a blueprint model of school reform. In fact, staff at Henry Louis realize that blueprints don't work well if principles of intrinsic motivation are to guide comprehensive school reform. For adults to value and implement new ideas in their classrooms, they must value and experience them in their own lives.

To encourage the first two conditions of the motivational framework (inclusion and a positive attitude toward learning), the school is the locus of control. Teachers, parents, and administrators adapt ideas to their own context and elaborate upon them in ways that reflect their imagination and sense of efficacy. To encourage the third and fourth conditions (enhancing meaning and engendering competence), adults regularly engage in reflective practices such as peer coaching and action research. In this way learning is interesting and challenging, and it contributes to concrete ways to identify success. These are the principles articulated within the motivational framework, Henry Louis's schoolwide pedagogical language.

Henry Louis Elementary School used year one (see Exhibit 1.2, p. 29) to experiment with lesson design using the motivational framework in grade-level planning teams. In addition, the school hired a rotating substitute to free teachers to visit each other's classrooms to observe the ways in which school-based expertise already supports student motivation. This helped teachers more deliberately access existing expertise. This was also a time when teachers supported each other on ways to address existing challenges. For example, a teacher might have asked a colleague to observe a new teaching strategy and its influence on a child who has been particularly difficult to reach.

Toward the latter part of the school year, the external consultant met with grade-level teams, shadowed by the school renewal coach, the principal, and the district liaison. Although the consultant had been working off-site to develop the expertise of the renewal team as school-based professional developers, these team meetings provided an opportunity for staff to interact with the external support, addressing concerns and fortifying understandings. They also served as a key opportunity to plan a motivationally anchored lesson with the coach and to observe its implementation. Each grade-level team provided feedback on the external consultant's demonstration lesson using the rubrics for the motivational framework (Ginsberg and Wlodkowski, 2000). With an agreed-upon protocol of warm feedback and cool feedback (*warm feedback* is what one might say to help a dear friend feel good; *cool feedback* is a bit more distant and focused on sharing collegial knowledge) and closing with goal setting and a date to follow up, staff members practiced coaching each other in a respectful and informative manner by coaching the external consultant.

The year concluded with Henry Louis Elementary School's first annual poster conference. A poster conference is a display of professional accomplishments that encourages the sharing of best practices among teachers. This provided an opportunity for teachers to make their learning explicit and to communicate it to the entire school community, in much the same way students might engage in assessment through exhibitions and demonstrations (Ginsberg and Wlodkowski, 2000).

Building on the foundation of the first year, the school's leadership team hosted a retreat. Faculty were able to strengthen their understanding of the motivational framework, develop sample lessons, examine challenges related to school change, and provide input into year two.

Year two included the following:

- Strengthening the focus of grade-level meetings with an agreed upon but uniform planning format

- Sharpening the focus of classroom visits

- Examining student work

- Initiating a demonstration portfolio process

A large part of Henry Louis's success, like the success of other schools renewing themselves with a focus on student and adult motivation, reflects the participants' sense of community as learners, their spirit of invention, and their courage to challenge themselves as adult learners. Successful schools are serious about examining data to become not only increasingly sensitive toward but effective with a broad range of students. Like Henry Louis Elementary School they form a sense of community, not through an isolated set of trust-building activities but through strategies that build trust while focusing on the ultimate goal: learning experiences that ignite student motivation and success.

As most educators realize, the pressure for higher standards and greater measures of accountability are often inspired as much by political self-interest as by a genuine concern for schools and the children and communities to which they belong. Nonetheless, across the nation, innumerable sincere and inspiring schools serve as examples of what it takes to keep the dream of strong public education alive. When we look closely at what adults are learning and doing, we consistently see principles of intrinsic motivation at work.

Activity One: Introducing Lesson Design with the Motivational Framework

Purpose   For educators to enhance and apply their understanding of motivationally anchored instruction to a daily lesson

Participants   Renewal team and other members of the school community

Time   Flexible

Format   Minilecture and experiential activities

Materials   An overhead transparency with a blank and completed motivational framework lesson-design format (Exhibits 1.1, p. 28 and 1.6, p. 35, respectively)

Process   Review with participants the four motivational conditions. Mention that the design format is for preplanning. The implementation rubric, known as the partnership guide for culturally responsive teaching and learning, provides additional support for implementing and reflecting on the design format (see Exhibit 1.3, pp. 30–32).

On a blank motivational framework lesson design format, ask participants to join you in mapping a sample lesson, based on something that a participant teaches. As an alternative, use the linear motivational framework lesson design format (Exhibit 1.4, p. 33) to map the agenda for the learning experience you are facilitating. Indicate where participants might locate strategies on the blank motivational framework. Participants will see that several of their approaches fit more than one condition. Encourage them to select the condition that seems most appropriate for each approach. Ultimately, the goal is to ensure that participants have addressed all four conditions and work together to support learning goals. The goal is not to use the framework to transform the motivational conditions into a contrived and fragmented set of activities.

Next, show participants (in storytelling fashion) a single lesson created with the motivational framework for a K–12 classroom. It is often interesting, and sometimes amusing, to do this with a demonstration lesson the facilitator has actually taught. Participants typically enjoy learning about the successes and challenges of an adult educator who is trying to practice what she or he teaches. Examples of elementary and middle school lessons are provided in Exhibits 1.5 and 1.6.

The middle school lesson exemplifies how application of the framework might look in a math classroom. The elementary school lesson, provided by Patty Gallegos, provides a motivationally anchored plan for a first-grade lesson in language arts and social studies. A high school lesson chronicles a block-schedule eleventh-grade social science class at a large urban high school in case study format.

• • •

High School Sample Lesson Plan

This plan will give you an example of how to put the motivational framework into action. It refers to the four questions in Exhibit 1.4.

Description   The blame cycle

Goals   To help students understand what blame is, how it works, and what we can do to control the tendency to blame; to develop higher-order thinking skills through a reframing exercise that helps people look at something that is a problem for them in a new and more positive way; to diminish the tendency to blame

Process

Establishing inclusion: The group works to answer the question: How does this learning experience contribute to developing as a community of learners who feel respected by and connected to one another and to the teacher?

Explain who you (the teacher or facilitator) are and why you are here.

Tell two wishes and a truth (Ginsberg and Wlodkowski, 2000, Chapter Five, Activity Two). Model for the class three things about yourself and ask them to guess which one is the truth.

Facilitate personal introductions. Ask each person to introduce him- or herself and to mention one thing about this school that people wouldn't know just by looking in.

Developing a positive attitude: The group works to answer the question: How does this learning experience offer meaningful choices and promote personal relevance to contribute to a positive attitude?

Provide an agenda to assure students that they will have a sense of choice in what they do.

Provide an overview of blame to develop relevance by helping students see that all people tend to attribute bad things that happen to forces outside of themselves. On one end of the spectrum, we say things like "It was a bad day" or "It wasn't in the stars." On the other end of the spectrum, we say things like "It's her fault" or . . ."He's a [blank]" (fill in the blank with a common label).

Ask students, in pairs, to think about why blame comes in so handy (for example, it lets us off the hook, gives us a sense of control, and provides a solution to complex problems).

Ask students, in pairs, to think of reasons why blame is a problem. Map the blame cycle using a personal experience (for example, my sons and I argue about the fact that they don't wear their coats in winter and what they tell me when they get sick). Ask students to map personal blame cycles. (For more information, see Ginsberg and Wlodkowski, 2000.)

Enhancing meaning: The group works to answer the question: How does this learning experience engage students in challenging learning that has social merit?

Explain that we are going to use a volunteer's blame-cycle map to interrupt the tendency to blame through a process called reframing. Ask for a volunteer who doesn't mind coming to the front of the room to share a blame map.

Demonstrate reframing, asking the entire class to think of all the positive reasons that the antagonist (or blamee) might have had for his or her actions. Chart the responses.

Ask the volunteer to select one of the class's positive "reframes" to work with. (It must be something the volunteer can honestly believe about the other person.)

Ask the class to brainstorm all of the things that the volunteer could do, knowing about this more positive way to understand the antagonist's behavior.

Ask the volunteer to select a course of action based on all of the options the class has provided.

Engendering competence: The group works to answer the question: How does this learning experience create students' understanding that they are becoming more effective in authentic learning they value and perceive as authentic to real-world experience?

Ask students to work with a partner to repeat the reframing process, using either partner's blame-cycle map.

Work with the group on blame similes: blame is like a [blank] because [blank]. (For example: blame is like a freight train because it runs down anything in its path.)

Ask the closing question: How might you use the blame cycle outside of this classroom?

• • •

Activity Two: Using Prior Experiences to Learn the Four Conditions of the Motivational Framework

Purpose   For educators to clarify ways in which "no-fail" lessons that they already use are consistent with the motivational framework

Participants   Members of the school community working in groups of five (grouping by subject or grade level works well the first time)

Time   One hour

Materials   Handout of Exhibit 1.3 or 1.4

Process

Step one: Begin by referring to a previous learning activity that includes all four motivational conditions.

Step two: Provide a handout based on the four conditions of the motivational framework, thus providing prompts and clues for all participants. Ask four volunteers to join you in front of the group. One represents the two criteria for inclusion; one represents choice and personal relevance for attitude; one represents the two criteria for meaning; and one represents the last condition, engendering competence. Narrate a successful lesson from your own experience that illustrates the criteria for the motivational framework but never use the names of the four conditions. Then, in round-robin style, ask each volunteer to tell you and the rest of the group how the learning experience you described met the criteria she or he represents. Facilitate a large-group discussion afterward to emphasize and elaborate insights from this round-robin process.

Step three: Ask participants to form groups of no more than five people in which they will repeat the process they have just observed. They begin by taking some time to reflect on learning activities they already use that meet all four conditions of the motivational framework. Each person takes a turn to share his or her example, and the four other participants assign criteria to themselves and offer feedback on the condition each represents. By rotating the role of teacher, each participant can give and receive reciprocal teaching or feedback about a learning experience in his or her own subject area. (Adapt this step for administrators and other group members who are not classroom teachers. For example, an administrator can use the example of a successful meeting.) The entire process should be very supportive, with everyone having a chance to apply and refine his or her understanding of the four motivational conditions.

Note: This round-robin activity can be used for different teaching purposes when a teacher wants to facilitate the sharing of different perspectives for commonly experienced phenomena. For example, students might listen to or read about a historical event and offer different perspectives on various characters (father, mother, child), political views (Republican, Democrat, Green Party), or ethnic groups (Latinos, Chinese Americans, African Americans); science students might review an ecological event and offer a possible analysis from the perspective of chemistry, biology, or physics.

Activity Three: Applying the Motivational Framework to an Upcoming Lesson

Purpose   For educators to apply their understanding of the motivational framework to a standard (or set of standards) they will teach

Participants   Members of the school community working in pairs or small groups (subject- or grade-level-specific groups work well the first time)

Time   Flexible

Materials   An overhead transparency with the motivational framework template, a blank transparency of the framework (Exhibit 1.1) for each small group, transparency pens

Process

Step one: Identify the concept or standards to be learned.

Step two: On a blank template of the motivational framework, brainstorm ideas, using any of the motivational conditions as an entry point.

Step three: Assure that the group has addressed all four conditions of the framework, even though the focus may be on a specific condition because of the work that students have already done or will do in the next few days. Clarify that a single strategy may address more than one motivational condition and that mapping a lesson requires that you place the strategy where it seems to make the most sense. (The motivational framework is a guide; it is more a compass than a scientifically constructed map.)

Terri McLaughlin, a math coordinator, and Belinda Rendon, a middle school math teacher, for Spring Branch Independent School District in Houston, Texas, contributed this example:

Standards: Review the metric system and the customary system.
Approach: Terri and Belinda brainstormed ideas. These ideas follow.

> *Put up a life-size picture of the seven-foot-four-inch Houston Rockets basketball player from China, Yao Ming (developing a positive attitude). Facilitate carousel graffiti, as described in the example, to help students recall what they already know (developing a positive attitude). Graffiti questions and activities might include the following:*
>
> - *What do you know about the metric system of measurement?*
> - *What do you know about the customary system of measurement?*
> - *List some examples of things that measure about one centimeter.*
> - *List some examples of things that measure about one inch.*
>
> *Have students work together in groups of three to rotate around the room as they respond to each question that is posted on newsprint, one question per each piece of newsprint (inclusion). Ask students in small groups to share ways they can convert inches to centimeters; for example, they could calculate Yao Ming's seven feet four inches to centimeters by converting the seven feet to inches first, then adding four more inches (enhancing meaning and engendering competence). Ask students to estimate and calculate, compare their own height in centimeters and inches (enhancing meaning). Ask students to do the same for Yao Ming (enhancing meaning). Ask students to compare calculations of their height with those for Yao Ming's height (enhancing meaning). Put students' calculations on an overhead transparency and look for patterns (developing a positive attitude and enhancing meaning). Ask students how well they estimated their own height in centimeters and inches. Ask them for their estimation strategies (enhancing meaning and engendering competence). Ask students to write on a three-by-five-inch card something that they learned and something that surprised them from today's lesson (engendering competence).*

Exhibit 1.6 (p. 35) illustrates how Terri and Belinda's lesson plan connects to the motivational framework for culturally responsive teaching.

Activity Four: Using a Case Study to Exemplify the Motivational Framework for Course Design

Purpose   To examine what an elementary, middle, or high school classroom might look like when it is implementing the four conditions of the motivational framework; to deepen understanding of the framework by applying knowledge about the four motivational conditions

Participants   Individuals and large group

Time   Twenty minutes

Materials   Case studies

Process   Ask participants to read one of the following case studies and to be prepared to answer one or more of the following questions:

From your perspective, what are the best examples of how the teacher in the case study applies the four conditions of the motivational framework?

If you were the teacher, what else might you do?

If you were coaching the teacher, how might you provide support to help your colleague strengthen his or her practice?

What insights, challenges, or new areas to explore occur to you as a result of analyzing this case study?

Note: Aspects of these case studies were adapted from Ladson-Billings (1994) and Shade, Kelly, and Oberg (1997).

• • •

Beverly Hillman, Teacher (Middle or High School Example)

Beverly Hillman has been teaching social studies for four years at Jefferson High School, a large demographically mixed school in Chicago. The school is trying to recognize the talents of all students and create the motivational conditions to support their success. Beverly regards herself as a conscientious teacher with a very challenging job.

Beverly's classes are two and one-half hours long because of Jefferson High School's block teaching schedule. She begins each class with fifteen-minute cooperative base groups. The purposes for group meetings vary, but a primary goal is to ensure respectful and productive peer support for all students. Beverly has worked with students so that each base-group member always has a clearly defined role, for example, facilitator, timekeeper, recorder, reporter, or process observer. Beverly has also worked with students to create consciousness about agreed-upon norms for collaboration and, in particular, positive ways to encourage all group members to participate in base-group dialogue. Today's base-group task is to solve problems that students may have had with last night's homework. Yesterday's task was to share notes from the previous class session and identify three key insights.

Beverly organizes all of her teaching around problems and issues. For example, ninth-grade students are studying how cities develop. The students have studied cities in ancient African kingdoms, Europe, and Asia. They have taken trips to city hall and have seen the city council in action. In fact, the mayor has visited their classroom. Groups of students have worked on solutions to problems specific to their city. The problems included the city's budget deficit, homelessness, the poor condition of the roads, and crime. Students wrote letters to the editor of local papers and presented their recommendations to different community representatives and task forces.

Each student is becoming an "expert" in some aspect of urban living. For example, students are studying the city's architecturally unique buildings, bridges, urban planning, recycling programs, schools, and the contributions and challenges of local artists. Every Tuesday, instead of coming to class, students work in teams with a community mentor who teaches them about the mentor's area of expertise.

Students are working toward an exhibition night so that they can demonstrate to their parents, mentors, and other community members what they have learned. Students will create multimedia presentations to use and develop strengths in their multiple intelligences. They are also keeping a process-folio, similar to a portfolio, that chronicles their experiences, research, and contributions. Twice a month Beverly meets with students individually to review process-folios and to refine and update individual goals.

Students understand Beverly's scoring system for all of their assignments:

- A score of four means "Outstanding job! You could teach this."
- A score of three means "Good. You are almost there."
- A score of two means "Practice some more. You can do it on your own with more attention to detail."
- A score of one means "Ask for help so that once you practice some more, you are going to really understand."

For their presentations about their city, students will be rated on criteria such as knowing information in depth; speaking clearly and being easy to understand; using visuals and other props; demonstrating clear organization with introduction, major points, and summary; staying focused; and using creativity in style of presentation. Beverly hopes that her assessment will work to guide students' learning as well as assess it. She is hopeful about their accomplishments because she has found that when students learn in ways that are natural to them, they experience increased academic achievement and confidence in themselves as learners and as people.

Regularly, Beverly talks or meets with parent volunteers who have been helping to coordinate the community mentor program. Parent volunteers also work with students to produce a monthly newsletter related to community issues and their learning experiences. Along with students, parents are working with a technology specialist to post a state-of-the-art newsletter on the Internet, using imaginative applications.

Next year, when students are in tenth grade, they will do a presentation for ninth graders to share what they learned and to encourage the new ninth-grade students to reach beyond their dreams.

• • •

Bill Hollins, Teacher (Elementary School Example)

Bill Hollins is a second-grade teacher at New Horizons, a demographically mixed urban school. The school is trying to recognize the talents of all students and create the motivational conditions to support their success. Bill is in his ninth year of teaching and regards himself as a conscientious teacher with a very challenging job.

Bill starts each day by greeting each student at the door. After putting their name cards in the attendance bucket, students sit in a circle for a class meeting. Bill always uses this time to do three things: (1) recall the previous day's learning focus; (2) recall significant activities, events, ideas, values, and assignments; and (3) use group responses, calls, and claps to heighten the level of group participation in learning. In addition, he involves the whole group in acts of remembering, affirming, and valuing individual and group learning. Sometimes he initiates a group activity that helps students know more about each other and learn to work together well. Students play name games, use concentric "inside-outside" circles to talk to each other, talk about how to handle put-downs from other people, tell a group story to learn to rephrase what the speaker before them said in order to practice being good listeners, and make gumdrop inventions to practice cooperative group skills. As much as possible, Bill shares the spotlight with his students so that each student has a chance to lead the class meeting. He uses the word *griot* (pronounced gree-o, a West African word for an expert in oral performance) for the student-leaders. On Mondays, Bill reviews the class agreements that are focused on self-respect and respect for others, responsibility (taking care of oneself and others), imagination (imagining goals, planning for them, being persistent), effort, and positive humor.

At the end of the day, Bill asks students to make a circle, close their eyes, and visualize their day and their completed tasks. He then asks them to talk about what they learned that they are going to talk about at home or what they hope to learn more about because of something that happened today. Students write or draw their ideas on a door pass that they give to Bill as they leave, giving Bill a chance to say good-bye to each student.

Bill also asks students to accept responsibility for classroom organization and management. For a five-day period, students assume such roles as receptionist, timekeeper, courier, distributor of work and materials, collector of work, room inspector, pet and plant care specialist, and chalkboard maintainer. Students evaluate their performance on these roles through goal sheets, journal entries, and pre- and postevaluations.

Along with creating a safe and responsible environment for learning to occur, Bill believes in strong affective support for academic learning. He uses small-group learning, peer tutoring, and heterogeneous grouping to build a family atmosphere. In addition, word tasks and instruction provide opportunities for students to express themselves creatively, learn about the culture and traditions of all of the people in the United States—and the world, and explore the community. Because the students like it when Bill plays music while they work, Bill does so regularly.

Bill is also creative with reading and writing. He has had students slide around the room to demonstrate how some letters and sounds blend together. Students then slide letters and sounds together. Bill also uses choral reading, singing, call-and-response techniques, demonstrations, and performance as well as kinesthetic instruction. This is good for all students, but it is especially helpful to students who are new to the English language.

To help students appreciate and comprehend literature, Bill involves them in writing, acting, and drawing some of the ways they are like and different from a character in a book. Students have also written letters to a character in the book, and then they have pretended that the character writes back by taking turns responding to one another's letters. Students have also written about something that they have made up about a character that others don't know. And at times students have written, drawn, and role-played characters' perspectives on a topic. Regardless of what students are learning and doing, they can see their work proudly displayed around the room, alongside of which Bill posts the content standards that the work exemplifies.

When it comes to assessment, Bill works hard to provide opportunities for students to demonstrate what they have learned with a clear understanding of what success looks like. His scoring system is the following:

- A score of four means "Outstanding job! You could teach this."
- A score of three means "Good. You are almost there."

- A score of two means "Practice some more. You can do it on your own with more attention to detail."

- A score of one means "Ask for help so that once you practice some more, you are going to really understand."

For a storytelling unit, Bill recently rated students on criteria such as knowing information in depth; speaking clearly and being easy to understand; using visuals and other props; demonstrating clear organization with introduction, major points, and summary; staying focused; and using creativity in style of presentation. Before they began creating and telling stories, students worked with Bill to understand what each of the criteria looks like. As with most major assignments, he distributed goal cards, on which he had students set personal goals, develop a brief plan to accomplish them, and identify a peer coach to assist with challenges. In all subjects Bill tries to use real-life situations that are connected to students' experiences to help them create a product or demonstration. This approach guides learning as well as assesses learning. Bill has found that when students learn in ways that are natural to them, they experience increased academic achievement and confidence in themselves as learners and as people.

Source: Aspects of both cases adapted from Ladson-Billings (1994) and Shade, Keller, and Oberg (1997).

Activity Five: Implementation Rubrics Based on the Motivational Framework

(*Note:* Application of the peer coaching and data-in-a-day rubrics to a personal lesson is detailed in Chapter Three.)

Purpose   For educators to reflect on the implementation (as opposed to the design) of a lesson in a nonthreatening manner

Participants   Cadre or members of the school community working in small-group cooperative-learning jigsaw (with each member representing a different motivational condition)

Time   Forty-five minutes

Materials   A video of a brief teaching segment or a set of clips such as the ones used in the video *Good Morning Miss Toliver* (1993); handout of a complete set of rubrics for each participant

Process

   Step one: Distribute a copy of Exhibit 1.1. Explain that the handout is a synthesis of the research on educational equity, opportunity, and intrinsically motivating teaching. This is what educators who are committed to highly motivating, culturally responsive teaching would consider and, ideally, facilitate as they plan and implement learning experiences. Next, explain that you will be showing a video of a lesson. Ask participants to use Exhibit 1.3 (p. 30), the partnership guide, to note the strengths of the lesson as well as any ways to elaborate on it to enhance the four motivational conditions.

Step two: After participants review a half-hour teaching segment, have them discuss their findings either with a partner or in small groups. They should note strengths and ways in which the lesson might be motivationally enhanced and suggest ways in which they might communicate their findings to the "colleague" in the video. After about fifteen minutes, ask the participants to come back together as a large group. Ask participants to pretend that you (the facilitator) are the person in the video. (This will already be true if you have facilitated demonstration lessons in actual classrooms and videotaped them for later examination with school-based educators.) Participants provide feedback based on the video performance. They communicate their observations to you and one another in ways that are respectful and encouraging. If they word comments in ways that could impede trust or affect your ability to consider what they are saying, simply say, "Ouch." The deliverer of the message will then have an opportunity to rephrase the observation. (The deliverer may ask for assistance from others.)

Finally, basing your remarks on the feedback, articulate and commit to one or two goals that have arisen from the group, to enhance student motivation in future practice. Also define how you will garner support for the goals. For example, if a goal is to offer equally rigorous choices from which collaborative student groups may select, the community might garner support by sharing such a lesson plan with a skillful colleague and a focus group of students.

Step three: Debrief. Ask participants to set three goals for themselves. The first goal is to devise one or two ways in which they might strengthen their own classroom practice, given what they may have learned about themselves from observing someone else. The second goal is to articulate one or two ways in which they will strengthen their potential as an effective peer coach. The third goal is to decide when and how they will videotape a lesson or invite a trusted colleague to their own classroom to observe. Ask the group to report on ways to be an effective coach, and have someone transcribe the tips and distribute them later for future use. On three-by-five-inch cards and self-addressed postcards, have participants write goals related to strengthening their own practice and videotaping or inviting another person to observe a lesson. (Tell participants to have fun with their postcards, offering themselves encouraging comments and other uplifting thoughts.) Collect the index cards for future reference and mail the postcards to participants as a reminder.

EXHIBIT 1.1

The Motivational Framework for Culturally Responsive Teaching

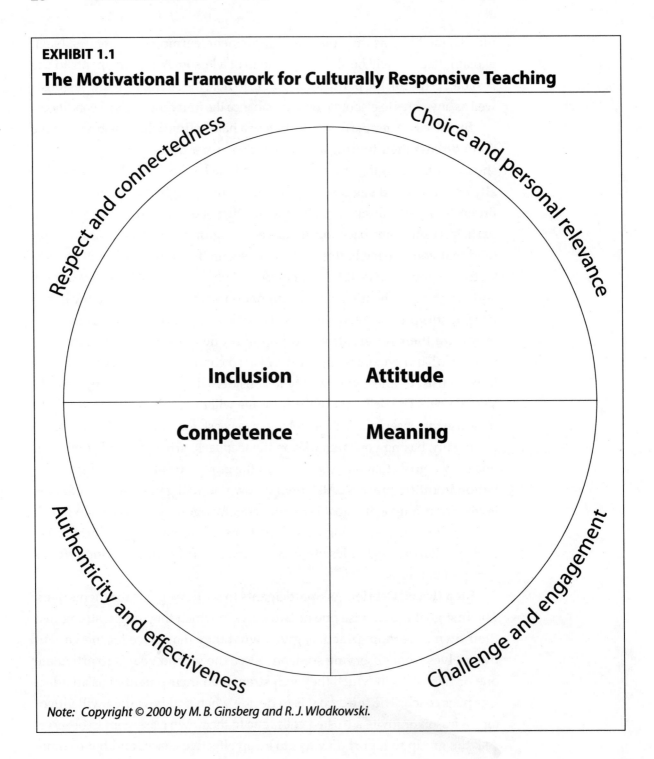

Note: Copyright © 2000 by M. B. Ginsberg and R. J. Wlodkowski.

EXHIBIT 1.2

Henry Louis Elementary School: Year One

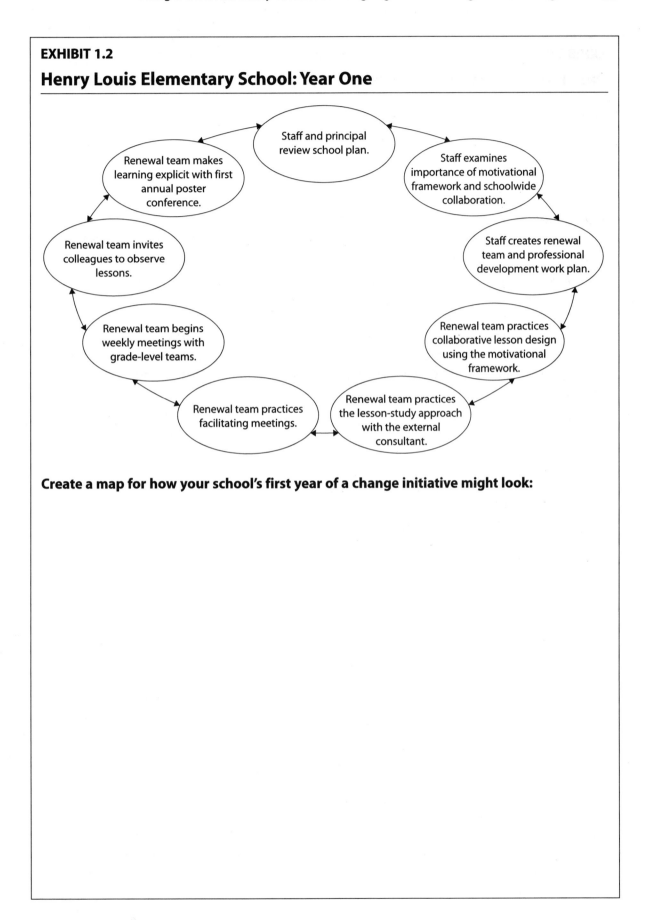

Create a map for how your school's first year of a change initiative might look:

EXHIBIT 1.3

Partnership Guide for Culturally Responsive Teaching and Learning

DESCRIPTION OF LESSON OR UNIT, SUBJECT AREA(S), AND GOALS:

_____

_____

_____

_____

Establishing Inclusion

How does this learning experience contribute to developing as a community of learners who feel respected by and connected to one another and to the teacher?

Routines and rituals are visible and understood by all:

_____ Rituals are in place that help everyone feel that they belong in the class.

_____ Students and teacher(s) have opportunities to learn about each other.

_____ Students and teachers(s) have opportunities to learn about each other's unique backgrounds.

_____ Classroom agreements (or rules) and consequences for violating agreements are negotiated.

_____ The system of discipline is understood by all students and applied with fairness.

Evidence: _____

_____

_____

_____

_____

All students are equitably and actively participating and interacting:

_____ Teacher directs attention equitably.

_____ Teacher interacts respectfully with all students.

_____ Teacher demonstrates to all students that she or he cares about them.

_____ Students talk to each other, work with a partner, or work in small groups.

_____ Students respond to a lesson by writing.

_____ Students know what to do, especially when making choices.

_____ Students help each other.

_____ Student work is displayed.

Evidence: _____

_____

_____

_____

_____

Developing a Positive Attitude

How does this learning experience offer meaningful choices and promote personal relevance to contribute to a positive attitude?

Teacher works with students to personalize the relevance of course content:

_____ Students' experiences, concerns, and interests are used to develop course content.

_____ Students' experiences, concerns, and interests are addressed in responses to questions.

_____ Students' prior knowledge and learning experiences are explicitly linked to course content and questions.

EXHIBIT 1.3. *(continued)*

_____   Teacher encourages students to understand, develop, and express different points of view.

_____   Teacher encourages students to clarify their interests and set goals.

_____   Teacher maintains flexibility in pursuit of teachable moments and emerging interests.

Evidence: _____

_____

_____

_____

_____

Teacher encourages students to make real choices about the following:

_____   How to learn (multiple intelligences)

_____   What to learn

_____   Where to learn

_____   When a learning experience will be considered to be complete

_____   How learning will be assessed

_____   With whom to learn

_____   How to solve emerging problems

Evidence (use back of page, if necessary): _____

_____

_____

_____

_____

Enhancing Meaning

How does this learning experience engage students in challenging learning that has social merit?

Teacher encourages all students to learn, apply, create, and communicate knowledge:

_____   Teacher helps students to activate prior knowledge and to use it as a guide to learning.

_____   Teacher, in concert with students, creates opportunities for inquiry, investigation, and projects.

_____   Teacher provides opportunities for students to actively participate in challenging ways when not involved in sedentary activities such as reflecting, reading, and writing.

_____   Teacher asks higher-order questions of all students throughout a lesson.

_____   Teacher elicits high-quality responses from all students.

_____   Teacher uses multiple safety nets to ensure student success (for example, not grading all assignments, working with a partner, cooperative learning).

Evidence: _____

_____

_____

_____

_____

Engendering Competence

How does this learning experience create students' understanding that they are becoming more effective in authentic learning they value and perceive as authentic to real-world experience?

There is performance or product that supports students in valuing and identifying learning:

_____   Teacher clearly communicates the purpose of the lesson.

_____   Teacher clearly communicates criteria for excellent final products.

EXHIBIT 1.3. *(continued)*

_____ Teacher provides opportunities for a diversity of competencies to be demonstrated in a variety of ways.

_____ Teacher helps all students to concretely identify accomplishments.

_____ Teacher assesses different students differently.

_____ Teacher assesses progress continually in order to provide feedback on individual growth and progress.

_____ Teacher creates opportunities for students to make explicit connections between new and prior learning.

_____ Teacher creates opportunities for students to make explicit connections between their learning and the real world.

_____ Teacher provides opportunities for students to self-assess learning in order to reflect on their growth as learners.

_____ Teacher provides opportunities for students to self-assess their personal responsibility for contributing to the classroom as a learning community.

Evidence: _____

_____

_____

_____

_____

Note: Copyright © 1998 by Margery B. Ginsberg.

EXHIBIT 1.4

Motivational Framework Lesson Plan

Standard(s) or benchmarks(s): _____

_____

_____

How does this learning experience contribute to developing as a community of learners who feel respected by and connected to one another and to the teacher?

_____

_____

_____

_____

_____

Establishing inclusion:
respect and connectedness

How does this learning experience create students' understanding that they are becoming more effective in authentic learning they value and perceive as authentic to real-world experience?

_____

_____

_____

_____

Engendering competence:
authenticity and effectiveness

How does this learning experience offer meaningful choices and promote personal relevance to contribute to a positive attitude?

_____

_____

_____

_____

Developing a positive attitude:
choice and personal relevance

How does this learning experience engage students in challenging learning that has social merit?

_____

_____

_____

_____

_____

Enhancing meaning:
challenge and engagement

Other considerations: _____

_____

_____

EXHIBIT 1.5

Motivational Framework Lesson Plan: Sample First-Grade Lesson

Class: First-grade

Standard(s)or benchmarks(s): *Students compare and contrast the absolute and relative locations of people and places and describe the physical and human characteristics of places.*

How does this learning experience contribute to developing as a community of learners who feel respected by and connected to one another and to the teacher? *Teacher asks students what a neighborhood is. If no one is certain, explain that a neighborhood is where we live, shop, and sometimes work. Ask the students to think of all of the different things they see in their neighborhood. Students should mention their homes, school, stores, gasoline stations, parks, and so on. List their ideas on chart paper.* <div align="center">Establishing inclusion: respect and connectedness</div>	How does this learning experience offer meaningful choices and promote personal relevance to contribute to a positive attitude? *Ask students what they would like to learn about their neighborhood and what questions they have. Walk the students through the school's neighborhood. Students may take a pencil and notepad to jot down any landmarks they want to remember. Remind students to note whether any people are working in the streets and what they are doing.* <div align="center">Developing a positive attitude: choice and personal or cultural relevance</div>
How does this learning experience engage students in challenging learning that has social merit? *After the field trip, have students recall what they saw. What businesses exist in the neighborhood? Were people working? Was there a lot of traffic? Tape a large piece of butcher paper on the chalkboard. With the students' help, draw a map of the neighborhood. When finished, have students work in teams of four or five to make a three-dimensional model of their neighborhood, using milk cartons, construction paper, crayons, markers, Popsicle sticks, and so on. They may use the map on the board as a guide.* <div align="center">Enhancing meaning: challenge and engagement</div>	How does this learning experience create students' understanding that they are becoming more effective in authentic learning they value and perceive as authentic to real-world experience? *When students complete their projects, return to the list of questions they had before the field trip. See if they can now answer them. Ask students to draw a picture to show to their families about one thing they learned that they want to share.* <div align="center">Engendering competence: authenticity and effectiveness</div>

Other considerations: _____

_____

_____

Note: Patty Gallegos of Fremont Unified School District in Fremont, California, provided this lesson plan.

EXHIBIT 1.6

Motivational Framework for Culturally Responsive Teaching: Standards of Measurement

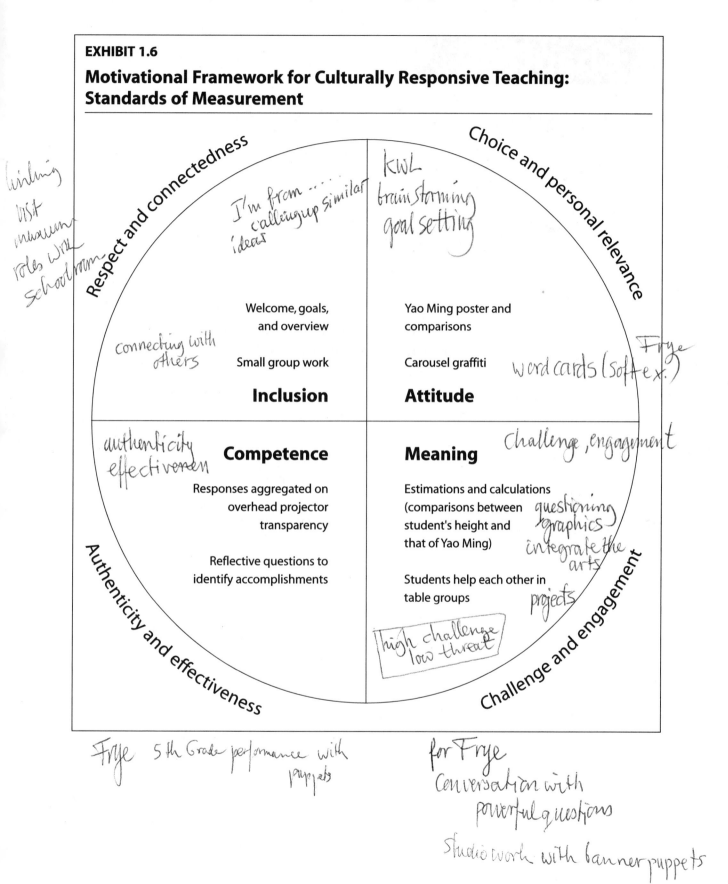

Handwritten annotations (clockwise from top left):

- (visiting museum roles with schoolroom)
- I'm from ... calling up similar ideas
- KWL brainstorming goal setting
- connecting with others
- word cards (soft ex.) Frye
- authenticity effectiveness
- Challenge, engagement
- questioning graphics integrate the arts
- projects
- high challenge low threat

Diagram text:

Respect and connectedness / **Choice and personal relevance**

Welcome, goals, and overview

Small group work

Inclusion

Yao Ming poster and comparisons

Carousel graffiti

Attitude

Competence

Responses aggregated on overhead projector transparency

Reflective questions to identify accomplishments

Meaning

Estimations and calculations (comparisons between student's height and that of Yao Ming)

Students help each other in table groups

Authenticity and effectiveness / **Challenge and engagement**

Handwritten notes at bottom:

Frye 5th Grade performance with puppets

for Frye
Conversation with powerful questions

Studio work with banner puppets

Chapter 2

Creating a Schoolwide Instructional Leadership Cadre

THE SCHOOLWIDE INSTRUCTIONAL LEADERSHIP CADRE (more simply the instructional leadership cadre or team) is the core of this kind of school renewal initiative. Cadre members are the first in the school community to learn the language of the motivational framework for culturally responsive teaching, personalize its potential, apply it to their practice, and cocreate ways to introduce it to the school community as a whole.

Sometimes a cadre is composed of members of the site-based leadership team or council. Frequently, however, it is a separate entity. Although safeguarding the centrality of instructional improvement is an essential responsibility for school-improvement teams, a range of responsibilities can distract site-based councils. An instructional leadership cadre helps the school maintain an instructional focus. Essentially, cadre members serve as the school-based professional development team that supports adult as well as student motivation. They do this through modeling, lesson studies, peer coaching, and ongoing study groups that focus on reflective practice.

Many school-change initiatives, especially those funded by the federal government, provide monies for a renewal coach, and this person, as explained in the job description for the coach (Activity Five of this chapter), coordinates the activities of the leadership team. In schools without a designated position for a coach, two leadership-team volunteers generally share the leadership. Schools may be able to find the monies for one or two teachers to serve part-time as classroom educators and part-time as leadership-team coordinators. In the absence of a leadership-team coach, a district liaison is encouraged to provide additional support to the principal.

A Positive Orientation Toward Change

In addition to enhancing a focus on instructional practice, a strong instructional leadership cadre helps establish a positive schoolwide orientation toward change. One of the greatest challenges to school renewal is resistance. Although resistance may be understandable, it can immobilize an initiative before it ever has a chance to take root. At times resistance occurs because of the central role schools are asked to assume in social change. The very notion of renewal can suggest that schools are being asked to redress social ills for which all of society ought to bear responsibility. As well, many educators are frustrated by mandates about which they have had minimal input. But this sentiment can prevail even when a school has voted to embark on a course of action. It is not uncommon for initial decision making related to how a school will approach a renewal process to involve a certain amount of deal making, such as a teacher's agreement to vote for an approach to schoolwide renewal as long as the approach does not require the teacher to change what he or she is already doing.

From a psychological perspective, resistance is associated with apprehensions about vulnerability or loss of control. This workbook, for example, advocates changing conventional teaching practices. However, many people have formed habits or expectations that run counter to various suggestions. To label as resistance their reluctance to participate or their failure to recognize the need to approach teaching and learning in different ways is usually ineffectual. It diverts attention from real goals and concerns such as providing greater emotional safety and greater clarity about learning goals and processes. Further, labeling adults, like labeling children, paralyzes hope and undermines creativity. As educators, we try to think of resistance as a call for enhanced clarity and support, as a means to more effectively address the process of school renewal.

At the same time, schools need to be able to move forward. Placing too much attention on concerns can bog down a transformation process and make it nearly impossible for a school to see results. This is a primary reason for working with an instructional leadership cadre. Most organizations, including schools, have a group of people who are absolutely committed to doing whatever the job requires. They are willing to apply a rigorous personal standard to the ways in which the organization sets and accomplishes shared goals. As well, organizations generally have a large group of people who care about good work but are cautious about the demands of change, even when it can lead to increased satisfaction. An example is busy parents who juggle the demands of work, children, and community activities.

In addition to these two groups of people, most school districts have a small number of people who are consistently negative. Their negativity works against posing critical questions that can help a school community to be more reflective. In many schools that have ceased to function as learning and growing communities, this sort of negativity has found an ear with a number of people who care about good work but are cautious about anything that makes additional demands on their time.

A cadre of credible instructional leaders can positively interrupt this phenomenon. They often inspire others in ways that even the most talented administrators cannot. Working side-by-side with strong leadership, a well-organized cadre plays an essential role in helping the school to excavate, focus, and mobilize internal expertise. They legitimize the potential for change and help a school stay the course long enough for transformation to develop a broad base of support.

Activity One: Constructing a Cadre

Purpose   To develop a team of teacher-leaders who can assist the entire faculty in maintaining and developing an instructionally focused approach to school renewal

Participants   The principal and representatives of the school community

Time   Flexible

Format   Dialogue with the school improvement team and informal dialogue with prospective cadre members

Materials   Handout describing the cadre's composition and duties (Exhibit 2.1, p. 45)

Process   Give the school community the text of Exhibit 2.1 to review. Discuss the guidelines and work toward agreeing to implement this approach to school renewal.

Activity Two: Creating a Statement of Purpose for the Cadre

Purpose   To define the purposes of the schoolwide instructional leadership cadre in ways that honor the perspectives of those who have been invited or volunteered to serve. (Note: This activity is best facilitated at an introductory work session with the cadre.)

Participants   Potential members of the cadre working as a large group

Time   Fifteen minutes

Materials   Handout of a draft statement of purpose (Exhibit 2.2, p. 47)

We have somewhere a statement of purpose?

Process

Step one: Ask cadre members, working individually, to review the draft statement of purpose (Exhibit 2.2). Request that they add to, delete from, and modify it as they desire.

Step two: Have participants share their recommendations as a recorder takes notes. Facilitate the process of reaching agreement on the changes that work well for everyone. Together, participants integrate agreed-upon changes into the new draft statement.

Activity Three: Encouraging the Leadership Cadre to Clarify Its Significance

Purpose To share common, different, and multiple perspectives about a particular topic in a way that activates prior knowledge and creates shared understandings as a foundation for learning.

Participants Leadership-cadre members working in both large and small groups

Time Forty-five minutes

Materials Newsprint, markers, and tape for posting carousel graffiti responses

Process The questions for this activity vary according to the purposes. The following example demonstrates how a school renewal facilitator can use this activity to build a positive attitude toward forming school-based teams of teacher-leaders and professional developers to support colleagues to develop motivating and culturally responsive instruction.

Is that happening?

Step one: Select approximately four questions from the following list that you believe to be most relevant to participants of schoolwide leadership cadres:

- How might having an instructional leadership cadre benefit your school?

- What might cadre members gain?

- How can the cadre members foster genuine collegiality between themselves and the rest of the school?

- What might a school want to know about itself to inform the process of creating and implementing schoolwide innovations?

- How can cadre members know if they are serving their school well?

- How might a school build commitment to imaginative and substantive continuous renewal?

- What might your school do to examine school renewal decisions and their impact on student learning and the school as a whole?

Step two: Using markers, write each of the questions you have selected for group dialogue across separate pieces of newsprint. Each piece of newsprint should contain only one question (that is, for four questions, use a total of four pieces of newsprint).

Step three: Ask members of the large group to count off so that they can form four small groups. (The number of groups must correspond to the number of questions selected.) When groups have formed, give each group a piece of newsprint with a question on it.

Step four: Explain to the groups that in just a minute they will be asked to collectively address their questions. The process is called graffiti because groups can record their responses to the question in any way they choose, including using symbols or other artistic representations, so long as others can understand their thinking.

After each group has had approximately five minutes to discuss and respond to its question, ask the groups to pass their question clockwise to the next group. Each group then considers its new question, adding to the previous group's graffiti. After five minutes, ask the groups again to pass their questions clockwise. This process continues until each group has had an opportunity to respond to all of the questions and has its own question back.

Step five: Ask all the groups to briefly summarize all of the contributions. Because all of the groups have had an opportunity to think about each of the questions, the summaries ought to be concise statements or artistic representations that express identifiable themes or draw a conclusion. Each group will need a reporter to share its group's summary, limiting the report to approximately two minutes. If space permits, post the graffiti responses around the room. Later, transcribe the information for further study.

Note: This activity works very well with students in mid-elementary through high school. For example, a teacher who is introducing a new book might use carousel graffiti (Exhibit 2.3, p. 48) with prediction questions.

Adapting Carousel Graffiti as a Way to Open Dialogue

Use the procedures for carousel graffiti with four or five of the following questions. Check first to ensure that all participants interpret the questions in the same way and that their interpretations are consistent with your own.

- What prevailing beliefs within your school or community reflect the dominant European-American culture and might be inconsistent with the experiences and values of staff or students from a variety of different backgrounds? (Examples of responses might be working alone or thinking primarily in terms of personal gain.)

- What is one valuable lesson you have learned—either directly or indirectly—from a person who is from a background that is different from your own?

- What are some attributes or components of schools in general that demonstrate respect for cultural pluralism?

- What is one lesson you have learned about a successful school renewal–planning process?

Activity Four: Creating an Initial Approach to Planning

Purpose   To devise an initial approach to working together as a team; to engage in initial planning that honors diverse perspectives

(Note: A variety of planning forms are provided in Chapter Three. The following form can be useful for initial decision making. This activity is best facilitated at the conclusion of an introductory work session with the cadre.)

Participants   Entire cadre working as a group

Time   Thirty minutes

Materials   Handouts of Exhibit 2.4 (p. 49) and 2.5 (p. 50)

Process   Ask cadre members to discuss and agree upon their responses to the questions in Exhibit 2.4. Fill out the alternative cadre planning form in Exhibit 2.5.

Guiding Questions for an Instructional Leadership-Cadre Team

The following questions can help a cadre make new learning explicit and initiate related activities.

- What have we learned from the work session?

- What is significant about what we have learned?

- What ideas do we want to implement first?

Activity Five: Defining the Role of the Coach or Leadership Chairperson

Purpose   To delineate the responsibilities of the coach or leadership chairperson so that all members of the cadre share expectations and agree on responsibilities from the start for this position; to safeguard against the temptation to turn the coach's job into a quasi-administrative position

Participants   Cadre working as a large group

Time   Fifteen minutes

Materials   Handout of Exhibit 2.6 (p. 51)

Process   Ask cadre members to review Exhibit 2.6 as a team. They may add to, delete from, and modify it as they desire.

Activity Six: Encouraging Self-Reflection Among Coaches

Purpose   To assist the coach in modeling a standard, to encourage regular self-assessment of personal beliefs and actions that contribute to motivationally effective school renewal. This self-assessment can stimulate regular goal setting for the coach, as well as for the leadership cadre.

Participants   Coach, principal, district liaison, and external consultant

Time   Thirty minutes

Materials   Handout of Exhibit 2.7 (p. 52)

Process   Ask the coach, principal, and district liaison to work as a team to review Exhibit 2.7. Request that they add to, delete from, and modify it as they desire. Ask each participant to use a scale from one to five (five = high; one = low) to assess his or her commitments and effectiveness. Share responses and ask each person to set two to three personal goals that can contribute to increased effectiveness. Set a review date to demonstrate the accomplishment of personal goals.

Activity Seven: Feedback on Leadership Sessions

Purpose   To heighten consciousness and skill related to applying the motivational framework to meetings and adult learning, as well as to classroom practice with students

Participants   Leadership cadre working as a large group

Time   Fifteen minutes

Materials   Handout of Exhibit 2.8 (p. 53)

Process   Ask cadre members to respond to Exhibit 2.8, rating the statements on a scale of one to five. Explain that their responses will be kept confidential and will be used to enhance the motivational effectiveness of future meetings.

An ongoing challenge for a school-based instructional coach is to actually focus on teaching and learning. The coaching position often becomes a quasi-administrative position. This is especially true in high-poverty areas where the stream of responsibilities a principal faces often defies imagination. The following approach to using the coach position can help identify and protect a coach's primary purposes.

Activity Eight: Planning with the Instructional Coach

Purpose   To support the instructional coach in focusing on specific daily goals to ensure his or her effectiveness in supporting a schoolwide reform initiative

Time   About fifteen minutes

Format   The daily planning process can be done on an individual basis; however, with the coach's permission, it can be much more beneficial if done with feedback from colleagues (principal, teachers, district liaison, and so on).

Materials   Handout of Exhibit 2.9 (p. 54)

Process   On a daily basis, the instructional coach should review his or her annual performance goals (for an example, see Exhibit 2.7, p. 52). The principal and coach should set these goals at the beginning of the year, paying special attention to the schoolwide improvement goals.

The coach should be involved in daily activities that effectively support improvement goals. Using the schoolwide improvement goals as a guide, the daily planning form in Exhibit 2.9 supports the implementation and attainment of these goals.

By planning on a daily basis and focusing on activities that support the school improvement goals, the coach is playing an instrumental role in supporting and implementing the schoolwide reform initiative.

Additional Strategies for Enhancing the Effectiveness of Leadership-Cadre Meetings

The following activities contribute to clear communication within a leadership cadre as well as with the school community. Although communication agreements and school plans are always "in progress," making assumptions and connections explicit is foundational to a positive and cohesive renewal process.

Activity Nine: Developing a Communication Agreement

Purpose   To provide an environment where people feel respected and able to share diverse perspectives

Participants   School staff working individually and in a large group

Time   Forty-five minutes

Materials   Handout of Exhibit 2.10 (p. 55)

Process   Individually, participants review the sample guidelines in Exhibit 2.10 and select, modify, and add other kinds of agreements that would assist in contributing to a positive and productive professional learning environment. If participants are classroom teachers, they also discuss recommendations for how to work with students to create similar agreements.

Useful resources for this activity are Hirsh, Delehant, and Sparks (1994); Champion (1993); Allen and others (1999); and Ginsberg and Johnson (1998).

Activity Ten: Creating a Graphic Aid for Linking and Maintaining School Goals

Purpose   To unify school goals in a graphic aid that helps members of the school community see how various commitments contribute to student motivation and learning

Participants   Instructional leadership cadre working as a group

Time   Thirty minutes

Materials   Handout of Exhibits 2.11 (p. 56) and 2.12 (p. 57)

Process

Step one: Explain that although the schoolwide renewal plan can be cumbersome, a graphic organizer can help members of the school community see how goals are interrelated and mutually supportive.

Step two: Distribute Exhibit 2.11 and ask the instructional leadership-cadre members what they like and what needs to be changed. As a team, review the school plan and customize the graphic aid to the school's beliefs and plans (Exhibit 2.12).

Step three: Develop a process to repeat the approach with the school as a whole. For example, some schools delineate strategies in the "classroom strategies" section to correspond with the motivational framework and support strong learning. Essentially, they comprise a set of "givens" that could be seen when visiting any classroom across grade levels and academic disciplines.

Summary

A large part of developing a successful leadership cadre is ensuring that cadre members are part of an environment in which they are respected by and connected to one another. They must agree on norms that create safety and acceptance in order for the cadre to manifest and learn from diverse values, perspectives, and ways of interacting. This not only diminishes the feelings of isolation that can deteriorate the motivation to learn, it establishes an environment that encourages people to take risks that are fundamental to innovation. Like their students, teachers who do not feel included are far more likely to guard their resources, strengths, and perceived weaknesses. Inclusion, therefore, is at the core of genuine empowerment, agency, and success—whether in the classroom, in a leadership-cadre work session, or at a staff meeting. Inclusion is fundamental to the strategies in this chapter and in this book. The following chapter elaborates on the notion of safety by providing concrete tools for substantive collaboration.

EXHIBIT 2.1

Cadre Guidelines

Cadre Composition

Ideally, instructional leadership cadres are composed of ten to fifteen members:

- One administrator (a standing member)

- One school-based initiative coach or leadership team chairperson (a funded position)

- One teacher from each grade-level or content area

- Representatives from the arts

- One representative from special education

- Representatives from federally funded programs such as bilingual education or Title I

- One school-based literacy specialist (It is not uncommon for high-poverty schools to have a literacy coach.)

- Three parent or community representatives

- One representative of support staff

- One district-office liaison with high-level decision-making authority

- One representative from the school improvement team

Time Period for Service

Representatives serve three-year or two-year terms so that approximately seven of the ten to fifteen positions are available for election or invitation each year. Generally, initial representation includes a fifty-fifty combination of volunteers who serve a three-year term and volunteers who serve a two-year term prior to a standard two-year rotation process.

What Leadership Cadre Representatives Need to Be Willing to Do

The leadership cadre works with colleagues to experiment with and adapt research-validated instructional strategies to the school's strengths and needs. Cadre members serve as expert learners, site-based professional developers, mentors of instructional improvement, and advocates of motivationally anchored and continuous school renewal.

Working in concert with a district-level team, which comprises the superintendent's staff, a cadre creates systematic structures for learning and action. Based on the district calendar and opportunities for external support, these might include capacity-building institutes, monthly (first year) or quarterly work sessions (often with a network of teams from other schools), weekly self-directed study groups for planning and reflection, school-based institutes, peer coaching, weekly small-group sessions with grade-level or subject-area colleagues, a personal process folio, and an end-of-the-year poster conference to support the school's commitment to motivation and learning among diverse students. (Ginsberg and Wlodkowski, 2000, delineates areas of expertise developed over time).

EXHIBIT 2.1 *(continued)*

Topics to Focus Learning and Decision Making
Chapter numbers that follow each item refer to Ginsberg and Wlodkowski (2000).

- Awareness of and commitment to a motivationally anchored, shared instructional language as a vehicle to support greater success among all students (Chapter Two)

- Importance of collaborative adult learning focused on continuous instructional improvement (Chapter Three)

- Adult learning structures that contribute to student achievement, for example, collaborative lesson design, peer coaching, lesson studies, examining student work, action research (Chapter Three)

- Use of conventional and creative data, especially as success relates to redressing the disparities in student performance indicated by district and teacher data (Chapter Four)

- Advocacy at every level of the system, including students whenever feasible (Chapter Five)

- Schoolwide agreement on and development of a signature or theme that can unify and ignite a school's vision (Examples of signature are community learning, integrating arts and literacy, and using inquiry to connect school and work.) (Chapter Five)

Reflections and suggestions for customizing your school's approach to continuous improvement:

EXHIBIT 2.2

Draft Statement of Purpose for the Cadre

The purpose of the schoolwide leadership cadre is to inform, demonstrate, and encourage your school to apply information and methods of instruction that respond to the needs and interests of all students. The cadre supports its school in applying the motivational framework to lesson and course design. In addition, it works with the school to create the conditions in which all students schoolwide experience the following:

- Respect and connectedness to each other and to their teachers

- Curriculum and instruction that is relevant, challenging, and engaging

- Assessment that is meaningful to students, promotes learning, and clearly identifies the ways in which students are becoming competent at what they value (and what is of value to their communities)

The leadership cadre will work with its school in a way that promotes positive involvement of all school community members (parents, school staff, students, and community members), helps build collaborative schoolwide norms, facilitates ongoing, job-embedded adult learning through the development of professional learning teams and peer coaching, and collects data so that the school can identify its accomplishments and make informed decisions for continuous schoolwide improvement.

Customize your own draft statement of purpose in the following space:

EXHIBIT 2.3

Carousel Graffiti

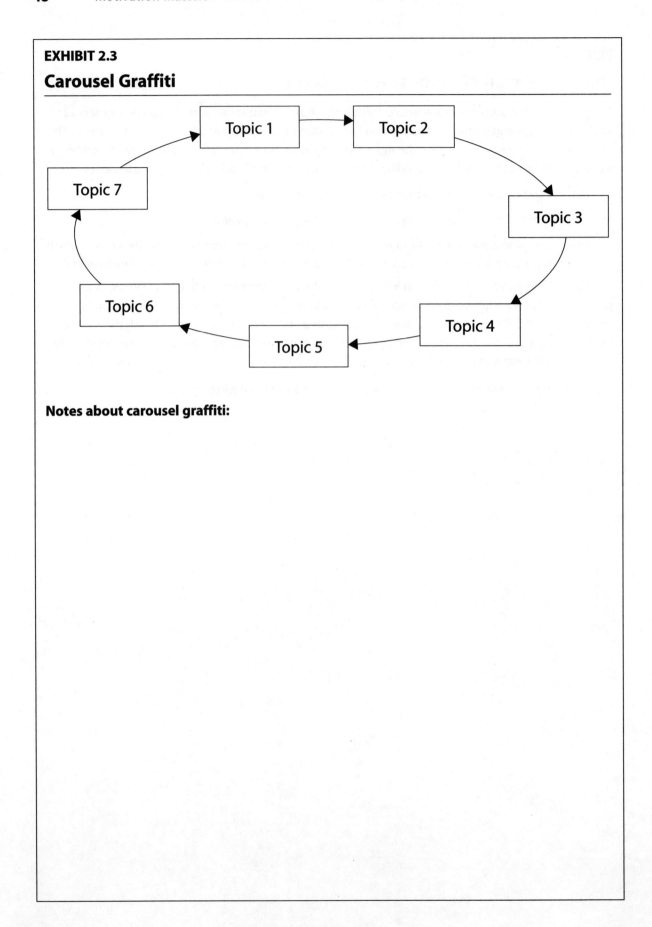

Notes about carousel graffiti:

EXHIBIT 2.4

Initial Cadre Planning Form

School: _____

Date: _____

Contact person: _____

1. How will the cadre find uninterrupted time to meet? _____
   _____
   _____

2. Given our work together thus far, what are some of our priorities related to creating highly motivating teaching and learning for all students? _____
   _____
   _____

3. What kind of an approach and approximate time line might help our school experiment with new approaches to teaching, strengthening collaborative adult learning, and assessing changes that occur because of this work? _____
   _____
   _____

4. How will our school ensure that decisions are made that directly and positively affect teaching and learning? _____
   _____
   _____

5. What kind of coordination and feedback loop needs to exist with the rest of the school and with existing committees and initiatives? _____
   _____
   _____

6. What roles will cadre members take on (for example, chairperson, recorder, time keeper, process observer, team member)? (The principal should serve as a cochair. See Chapter Four.) _____
   _____
   _____

7. How will we make decisions (for example, consensus, concordance, with or without a quorum of two-thirds of the team)? _____
   _____
   _____

8. How can we move ideas forward in a manner that respects urgencies but is fair to our school community? _____
   _____
   _____

EXHIBIT 2.5

Alternative Cadre Planning Form: Setting Up Our Learning Team

Instructions: You can use this cadre planning form for grade-level or subject-specific teams. Modify existing items or add new ones.

1. Agree on our reasons for working together.

2. Establish meeting logistics:
   - Meeting dates and times
   - Structure for meetings
   - Rotation of responsibilities for facilitation and recording
   - _____
   - _____
   - _____

3. Agree on team norms:
   - Start and end meetings on time.
   - Be open to learning from each other.
   - Avoid blaming or pointing fingers.
   - Avoid explanations or rationalizations.
   - Protect team time by staying focused on the outcomes.
   - _____
   - _____
   - _____

4. Practice ongoing collaboration:
   - Learn about and share research focused on motivationally anchored instructional practice.
   - Design lessons collaboratively.
   - Try new strategies and share the results.
   - Ask for help when you need it.
   - Analyze data and prioritize standards for the cadre to address.
   - Analyze student work and other forms of qualitative data.
   - _____
   - _____
   - _____

Notes: _____
_____
_____
_____
_____
_____
_____
_____
_____

Note: Adapted from the work of Jan Herrara of Adams Twelve Five Star Schools and the Thornton High School leadership cadre, Thornton, Colorado.

EXHIBIT 2.6

Job Description: School-Based Coach or Leadership-Team Chairperson

The job of a coach is to serve as an expert learner and supporter of motivationally anchored school renewal. This includes participating in and helping the instructional leadership cadre to facilitate school-wide (1) the design of motivating lessons, (2) instructionally focused grade-level planning, (3) lesson studies and peer coaching using the motivation framework, and (4) strategies for ongoing renewal that the school community prioritizes. In addition, the instructional coach will maintain a personal portfolio that documents the following:

- The design and implementation of a sample unit (four to five standards-based lessons in a volunteer classroom)

- A videotape and reflective narrative of one lesson conducted in concert with the district liaison

- Samples of student work that the instructional leadership team has shared to teach the process of examining student work

Customize a job description for a school-based coach or leadership-team chairperson for your school:

EXHIBIT 2.7

Self-Assessment for Coach and Leadership Cadre

I Believe	I Demonstrate	My School and I Take Action
I believe in a vision of motivationally anchored learning—for children and adults.	I model a vision of motivationally anchored learning—for children and adults.	I help others to develop a strong, shared vision of motivationally anchored learning.
I believe it is important for staff to address issues related to equity, such as respectfully listening to and responding to diverse interests, experiences and concerns.	I model ways to address issues related to equity, such as respectfully listening to and responding to diverse interests, experiences and concerns.	I facilitate ways for our school community to address issues related to equity.
I believe it is important to treat people with respect.	I facilitate in ways that encourage adults to treat each other with respect.	In my sessions, adults treat each other with respect.
I believe it is important for adults to regularly collaborate with one another in ways that support student learning.	I demonstrate processes for adults to regularly collaborate with one another in ways that support student learning.	I plan with adults so that they will regularly collaborate with one another in ways that support student learning.
I believe that adults are capable of producing high-quality work.	I try to find ways to help disengaged adults positively challenge themselves to teach in motivationally effective ways.	Adults throughout the school show that they are trying to strengthen the motivational effectiveness of their teaching.
I believe that it is important to use multiple forms of data to strengthen teaching and learning.	I demonstrate ways for teachers to use data to inform their work.	Collaborative groups of teachers regularly work to collect, assess, and take action based on data.
I believe it is important to help adults understand the process of change.	I find ways to help adults to positively understand the process of school change.	Adults throughout the school are willing to grapple with the complexity and occasional messiness of on-going school renewal.
I believe it is important for adults to demonstrate their expertise and learning.	I encourage adults to demonstrate their expertise and learning.	Adults throughout the school are willing to share their strengths.
I believe staff should be involved in the decision-making process that connects to our vision.	I model approaches for making fair decisions related to our vision.	Adults throughout the school make decisions that move us forward.

EXHIBIT 2.8

Feedback on Leadership Sessions

Instructions: Rate these statements on a scale of 1 to 5 (1 = strongly disagree; 5 = strongly agree).

The session climate was friendly and respectful (establishing inclusion).	1	2	3	4	5
This session was relevant to my work (developing a positive attitude).	1	2	3	4	5
This session challenged me to think (enhancing meaning).	1	2	3	4	5
This session helped me to be effective as a contributor to our school's vision of highly motivating classrooms. (engendering competence).	1	2	3	4	5
The facilitator respected the opinions and ideas of others (establishing inclusion).	1	2	3	4	5
In this session I was able to use my experiences and ways of knowing to support my learning (developing a positive attitude).	1	2	3	4	5
Most of the time during this session, I felt engaged in what was going on (enhancing meaning).	1	2	3	4	5
I will use the information or skills I have learned in this session (engendering competence).	1	2	3	4	5

Comments:

EXHIBIT 2.9

Instructional Coach Planning Form

Date:_____

Teacher or teacher group I'm working with: _____
_____
_____
_____

Professional development strategy (check as many as apply):

_____Lesson design

_____Lesson study

_____Peer coaching

_____Using data to plan

_____Data in a day

_____Development of grade-level assessments

_____Portfolio development

_____Rubric development

_____Action research

_____Demonstration lessons

Specific goals that today's strategies will help to support: _____
_____
_____
_____
_____
_____

Data supporting the use of professional development strategies: _____
_____
_____
_____
_____
_____

Action plan to support expected outcomes: _____
_____
_____
_____
_____

Notes for follow-up support: _____
_____
_____
_____
_____

EXHIBIT 2.10

Communication Agreement

A communication agreement comprises the guidelines and assumptions that govern how a group works together. By clearly identifying the kinds of interactions that group members will encourage and discourage, groups can create a climate of safety and respect.

In order to participate in a decision-making process in which everyone has to be able to live with the outcomes, the group must agree on some key points. The following ground rules provide a starting point for negotiation:

- Demonstrate respect for different opinions by listening carefully.

- Speak from your own experience, saying, for example, "I think" or "In my experience I have found" rather than generalizing experience to others, as in "People say" or "We believe."

- Diminish the tendency to blame.

- Honor the absence of others.

- Help maintain a problem-solving orientation to problems or disagreements.

- Work in a hopeful frame of mind.

- Help to keep the discussion on track.

- Speak to the whole group, as opposed to, for example, the facilitator alone.

- Share frustrations with the facilitator as a way of working toward positive change.

What modifications or additions might help to keep our work together today relevant and focused?

Add to, delete from, or modify the communication agreement to address your school's needs.

EXHIBIT 2.11

Sample School Organizer

School name: _____

Communication agreement

Classroom strategies

- Clear purpose
- Respectful interactions
- Peer collaboration
- Prior knowledge
- Students' experiences and opinions
- Choices
- Questioning skills
- Clear criteria for success
- Problem solving and projects
- Real-world assessment

Sequence of topics

- Communication agreement
- Motivational framework (all year)
- Collaborative teacher teams
- Data, examining student work
- Lesson studies (with warm and cool feedback)

School goals

- Attendance:
- Safety and respect:
- Reading:
- Writing:
- Computation:
- Science:
- Social sciences:
- Technology:
- Arts:
- Parent-family-community partnership:

Key components

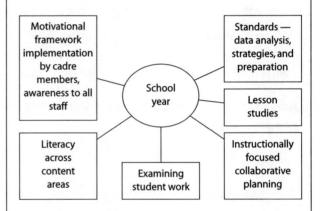

Descriptive data

EXHIBIT 2.12

Blank School Organizer

School name: _____

Communication agreement

Classroom strategies

Sequence of topics

School goals

- Attendance:
- Safety and respect:
- Reading:
- Writing:
- Computation:
- Science:
- Social sciences:
- Technology:
- Arts:
- Parent-family-community partnership:

Key components

School year

Descriptive data

Jan/III

Chapter 3

Implementing Motivating Strategies for Schoolwide Collaboration

EDUCATORS WORK WITHIN the constraints of a twenty-four-hour day. This is one of the reasons why a school with motivationally anchored instruction functions as a learning community rather than a collection of isolated teachers and classrooms. It would be nearly impossible for isolated professionals to develop expertise in every aspect of motivationally effective instruction. Professional exchange is important for the currency of ideas and commitment. In addition, many of the answers to educational challenges that educators face reside within the school. The challenge is to excavate, focus, and mobilize what is already known. This requires efficient processes, because collaboration needs to be an ongoing part of daily work in order to have its greatest impact. Random or superficial collaboration has minimal influence on strengthening teaching and learning.

This chapter provides several approaches to substantive collaboration. It begins with suggestions for finding additional time for constructing and sharing knowledge. Because Chapter Two, in introducing the motivational framework for culturally responsive teaching, provides several activities to facilitate lesson design, the focus of this chapter is a set of practices that support implementation of and reflection on new ideas. This includes peer coaching, lesson studies, and ways to work effectively as a team.

Who in our school collaborate successfully frequently
R. Cathy + Paula + Regina
2 Jill and Margaret
3 Connie + Salvica
young? age?
personalities?

Finding Time

The constraints that overwhelm professionals working in isolation are also a challenge for professionals working together. Consistently, educators ask: How will we find the time? Several resources can assist educators who seek to find time for collaboration. Raywid (1993); Murphy (1997); and Francis, Hirsh, and Rowland (1994) provide excellent examples of the ways that schools across the United States are successfully creating ongoing collaborative schoolwide learning among adults. Two issues of teacher-friendly journals also address the significance of adult collaboration and ways that schools are finding and using time with the goal of strengthening student learning: the summer 1999 issue of *Journal of Staff Development*, published by the National Staff Development Council, and the April 2001 issue of *Educational Leadership.* Several of the suggestions from these resources are included in the following activity.

Activity One: Creating Time for Collaboration (Professional Learning Teams)

Purpose   To encourage faculty to engage in collaborative planning, teaching, examination of student work, and other forms of reflective practice

Participants   School staff working in groups of three

Time   Thirty minutes

Materials   Handouts of Exhibits 3.1 (p. 67) and 3.2 (p. 68)

Process

   Step one: Ask school staff, in groups of three, to respond to the following questions and add any additional questions they would like to consider:

- What norms or traditional ways of organizing time make it challenging for adults in your school to learn and plan together?

- How do you currently tap into your colleagues' expertise?

- How might more flexibility with scheduling help members of your school community plan and work together in ways that support highly motivating classroom practice?

   Step two: Hand out Exhibits 3.1 and 3.2 to help staff consider ways to allocate time for enhanced collaborative learning. Ask staff, working in groups of three, to discuss the following questions: What is one idea you would like to try in support of greater collaboration? What would you need to do to make your idea a reality?

Classroom Support for Teaching and Learning

   In the past it was not uncommon to show teachers a presentation and expect them to implement it immediately on returning to their classrooms. Even when these presentations included experiential practice of new strategies and frameworks, we could not escape from this reality: if something is complex enough to matter, it is going to require support. If we are going to put classroom instruction at the center of school renewal, collegial interaction, grounded in the classroom, is essential. The following activities address this need.

Activity Two: Preparation to Use Peer Coaching
Based on the Motivational Framework

Purpose   To learn from classroom practice, as a teacher or peer coach, through analysis of a videotaped or real-time teaching experience

Time   Ninety minutes

Format   Interactive

Materials   Videotaped lesson (to practice peer coaching at a professional development institute), handout of partnership guide (Exhibit 1.3, p. 30) or data in a day (Exhibits 3.3 to 3.7, p. 69–73)

Process

   Step one: To practice using the motivational framework as a peer coach or to practice using it to review a videotape of one's own lesson, the professional development facilitator first distributes a copy of Exhibit 1.1 (p. 28).

   Step two: Explain that the handout is a synthesis of the research on educational equity, opportunity, and intrinsically motivating teaching. This is what educators who are committed to highly motivating, culturally responsive teaching consider and, ideally, facilitate as they plan and implement learning experiences.

   Step three: Explain that you will be showing a videotape of a lesson. Ask participants to use the handout to note the strengths of the lesson as well as ways in which the teacher might elaborate on the lesson to enhance the four motivational conditions. Explain that you will be practicing two kinds of feedback for each motivational condition: warm and cool. *Warm feedback* is what you might say to help a dear friend feel good; the focus is on all of the things that are good. *Cool feedback* is a bit more distant and focused on sharing collegial knowledge. Although respectful in tone, it suggests opportunities for strengthening the motivational effectiveness of a learning experience. Explain that participants will use cool feedback for setting personal goals at the end of the experience.

   Understandably, many teachers want to share only information that helps a colleague to identify strengths. Although this may be a good starting point, practicing both kinds of feedback is essential. Cool feedback is one of the best ways for teachers to remember how much collective information and imagination they share. The answers to some of our most puzzling motivational challenges often reside within the school; the key is to access that knowledge without everyone running for cover. The regular sharing of collegial knowledge can interrupt teachers' frustration and renew the spirit of invention.

   Step four: After participants review a half-hour teaching segment, they discuss their findings either with a partner or in small groups. They note strengths and ways in which the lesson might be motivationally enhanced, helping each other practice how they might communicate their findings to the "colleague" in the video.

Step five: After about fifteen minutes, the facilitator asks participants to come back together as a large group. He or she asks participants to pretend that the facilitator is the person in the video. Participants provide feedback to the facilitator based on the video performance. They communicate their observations to the facilitator-colleague in ways that are respectful and encouraging, noting both warm and cool feedback for each condition.

The facilitator or a scribe uses chart paper or an overhead transparency to note only the cool feedback for each of the four motivational conditions. (This helps keep the process efficient.) If the speaker words the feedback in ways that could impede trust or the ability of the facilitator to consider what is being said, the facilitator will simply say, "Can you help me understand that another way?" The deliverer of the message will then have an opportunity to rephrase the observation (and may ask others for help).

Step six: Based on the group's feedback, the facilitator articulates and commits to one or two goals to enhance student motivation in future practice. The facilitator also defines how she or he will garner support for the goals. For example, if a goal is to offer equally rigorous choices from which collaborative student groups may select, the faculty member might garner support by sharing such a lesson plan with a skillful colleague or a focus group of students. Finally, the facilitator identifies a colleague and a time line to share evidence of success or to discuss alternative ideas.

Step seven: Debrief. Participants set three goals for themselves. The first goal relates to one or two ways in which they might strengthen their own classroom practice, given what they may have learned about themselves from observing the colleague in the video. The second goal relates to one or two ways in which they will strengthen their potential as effective peer coaches. The third goal relates to when and how they will videotape their own lesson or invite a trusted colleague to their own classroom to observe (Exhibit 3.3). In addition, the group reports on ways to be an effective coach; have someone transcribe the tips and distribute them for future use. Goals related to strengthening one's own practice and videotaping or inviting another person to observe a lesson are written on a three-by-five-inch card and a self-addressed postcard. The facilitator collects the index cards for future reference and mails the postcards to participants as a reminder. (Encourage participants to have fun with their postcards, offering themselves encouraging comments and other uplifting thoughts.)

Note: To be effective, peer coaching needs to be regular and ongoing. Some schools use ideas from Activity One (finding time) to garner release time during the school day. One of the most practical approaches is to team

observing, coaching
but not
planning
lessons together
then.

with a colleague who has a planning period that is different from your own. That would make it possible, for example, for one person to visit the other person's classroom for thirty minutes every other Wednesday. The second person would visit the first person's classroom during his or her planning time on alternative Wednesdays. To compensate peer coaches for their time (acknowledging that this is at best symbolic because most teachers consistently exceed salaried hours), a teacher might leave immediately after students go home once a week.

Activity Three: Lesson Studies

Purpose   To develop awareness of the motivational framework, to apply data-in-a-day rubrics to a single lesson, to set the stage for teachers to videotape themselves and share their tapes to learn from classroom practice through analysis of a real-time teaching experience

Participants   Teachers in grade-level teams

Time   Ninety minutes

Format   Interactive

Materials   Blank motivational framework for lesson design (Exhibit 1.3 and Exhibits 3.4 to 3.7, p. 70–73)

Process

Step one: Divide into expert groups based on the data-in-a-day rubrics. Create one group for each condition of the motivational framework. Ask group members to review the rubric for their motivational condition and use the rubric to focus their observations as they watch the video.

The group focusing on inclusion will look for ways in which the teacher supports respect and connectedness. The group focusing on attitude will look for ways in which students are able to experience learning that is relevant and, to the extent possible, self-determined. The group focusing on meaning will look for ways in which the teacher on the video challenged and engaged students. And the group focusing on competence will look for ways in which students can plan for and identify their effectiveness and use authentic approaches to demonstrate learning.

Step two: Explain to each group that members will provide warm (or affirming) feedback and cool (constructive) feedback after observing a lesson.

Step three: Show the video (if possible, edit it in advance for efficient viewing) or model a lesson.

Step four: After observing a lesson, ask each group to share its insights. Chart each group's ideas for cool feedback.

Step five: Ask everyone present to set a goal for themselves, given a challenge they may be facing in reaching each and every student, and share goals.

Step six: Discuss next steps. Some examples are building videotaping into the next year's schoolwide plan, videotaping a teacher volunteer to practice this approach at the next faculty meeting, recruiting for a data-in-a-day experience at the end of the year, talking about how teachers might provide warm and cool feedback to each other when they visit each other's classrooms.

Activity Four: Quarterly Lesson-Study Days

George Middle School Instructional Leadership Cadre, Alum Rock, California, contributed this activity.

Purpose   To encourage teachers to observe each other's lessons, to enhance understanding of the motivational framework, to strengthen teaching and learning

Participants   Instructional leadership team members and teachers working individually and in small groups

Time   Thirty minutes

Materials   Blank motivational frameworks (Exhibit 1.1, p. 28) or note paper

Process

Step one: Members of the instructional leadership team volunteer to teach standards-based motivationally anchored lessons that address all four conditions of the motivational framework.

Step two: Rotating substitutes, the principal, and other staff free classroom teachers who have signed up in advance to observe a classroom.

Step three: Teachers who are observing jot down notes on either a blank motivational framework or on a sheet of paper with three columns: time, activities observed, comments or questions.

Step four: Observers are invited to join host teachers (teachers they have observed) for pizza and professional conversations during lunch. Each of the host teachers meets with colleagues at a designated location within a large room. Participants use the lesson-study approach from Activity Three to debrief the lesson.

Step five: Host teachers invite a colleague to offer a lesson for others to observe during the next round. Host teachers mentor their colleagues to provide support for designing a lesson with the motivational framework and to prepare for the pizza and professional conversations debriefing.

Activity Five: Establishing Norms for Teamwork

Purpose   To define how the schoolwide instructional leadership cadre or how a grade-level planning team will work together. Note: This activity is best facilitated at an introductory work session with the team.

Participants   Leadership team members working first as individuals, then triads, then teams of six. This activity can also include teams from several schools.

Time   Thirty minutes

Materials   Handout of Exhibit 3.8 (p. 74), sticky notes

Process   Participants review the handout of Exhibit 3.8 (p. 74), noting— on three different sticky notes (one idea on each)—the three most important things from the entire matrix that they need to have happen in order to effectively serve on the schoolwide leadership cadre. After a few minutes, individuals form triads, and the triads lay their sticky notes out on a tabletop and group them according to similarities.

Many items on the matrix could fit under several categories. For example, the theme of collaboration is represented in several different ways. Triads will easily find overlap among their priorities. Finally, the triad merges with another triad to become a six-person team. Team members repeat the process of grouping their priorities for common and distinct themes. They then prioritize their themes to identify the top three to five norms they would like to have in place. (Note: If staff developers are working with several schoolwide leadership cadres, they need to be sure that school-specific cadres work together.)

Next, the cadre members work together on a final statement that represents norms that will guide their teamwork. Finally, the facilitator asks the cadre (or cadres) to create a procedure for regularly assessing and strengthening their fidelity to their agreed-upon norms. They write their norms and procedure for assessing them on two three-by-five-inch cards, along with the names of two people who will serve as co-chairs for the cadre. They give one card to the facilitator and save one card for themselves.

Planning for Implementation of Staff Development Content

To sharpen and maintain the focus of a planning and learning team, grade-level or content-specific teams should modify the form in Exhibit 3.9 to fit their context and purposes. Many schools prefer to use the same agenda or meeting organizer throughout the building. Regardless, the process for customizing a form is the same. Ask faculty or faculty representatives to review Exhibit 3.9 (p. 77) entitled "Grade Level Agenda." Ask participants to underline what they like, modify what they would like to change, and draw a line through words or items they prefer to delete. After a brief discussion to review recommended changes, the leadership team or another faculty committee agree to meet within a brief period of time to create a new form that integrates faculty comments.

In several schools, all agendas also contain agreed upon norms. They serve as a reminder of faculty agreements regarding respectful and productive meetings and are briefly reviewed at the beginning of meetings. Upon concluding meetings, the norms are used to identify opportunities for enhanced collaboration. Often the facilitator will simply say, "How are we doing as a group and what can we do even better?"

Providing a space for everyone on the team to sign their name provides a record of who participated in the meeting. It also indicates agreement on outcomes. Schools determine such meanings when they create their agenda format. Shared decision making and responsibility for follow-through is the goal. The space for principal's comments provides a feedback loop.

Activity Six: Examining Student Work to Overcome Motivational Challenges

Purpose   To sharpen and maintain the focus on motivation and learning using a single piece of student work

Time   Forty-five minutes

Format   Small groups

Materials   Newsprint and markers for charting ideas

Process

Step one: The teacher on focus shares a piece of student work and identifies the standards she or he was hoping the student would master.

Step two: The team asks clarifying questions to strengthen understanding of the student as well as the scenario in which the work was produced, including how the teacher applied the motivational framework to (1) make learning safe, (2) create choices and relevance, (3) inspire challenge, and (4) provide concrete information about how success with this assignment would look and how students would share new learning in authentic ways.

Step three: The teacher on focus provides clarifying information.

Step four: The teacher agrees to remain silent and chart colleagues' ideas as the group brainstorms ways to address the challenge. One of the reasons that the teacher is asked to remain silent is to support the team in generating a broad range of ideas without feeling inhibited by the likelihood that the teacher may already have tried several of the ideas. In some instances uninhibited brainstorming can interrupt a person's sense of despair or frustration as colleagues boldly envision new opportunities.

Step five: The teacher on focus reviews the list of ideas with the team without passing judgment, then selects one or two ideas and sets concrete implementation goals. Team members also select one or two ideas and set related goals that may apply to their own situations.

Step six: The team, including the person on focus, reflects upon the process. The teacher on focus is encouraged to communicate feelings, thoughts, or ideas that can further a sense of respect and support for future collaborative work.

Activity Seven: Examining Student Work to Share Understandings About Proficiency

Purpose   To sharpen the team's focus on high-quality learning by sharing samples of student work

Participants   Teachers in learning teams grouped by grade level, department, or study group

Time   Forty-five minutes

Materials   Handout of Exhibit 3.10, p. 78

Process   Compare examples of student work (maximum of fifteen minutes). Organize examples of student work according to different levels of proficiency and identify next steps for each of those groups of students, including ways to strengthen the motivational conditions that influence learning. Set individual goals, including evidence you will share at the next meeting to exemplify accomplishments and challenges (Exhibits 3.11 and 3.12).

Exhibit 3.10 can serve as an organizing tool to document next steps and goals for each level of proficiency.

Note: An excellent resource for examining student work as well as other powerful designs in professional development is *Powerful Designs for Professional Development* (Easton, 2003).

Summary

Every learning activity, whether in a classroom or with adult learners, has to meet the four conditions of the motivational framework. When an activity does not go well, educators use the criteria to examine, refine, and improve it. Often, they do so with a trusted colleague. Many have learned to resist the temptation to simply throw away new ideas. Effectively using a new strategy generally takes a good deal of practice. This is a reason why collegial support is so important. As reasonably successful teachers, many of us have become self-protective. Whether we want to admit it or not, the need to look good, appear smart, and sound capable can overwhelm our own opportunities to learn. There is truth in the adage "No one of us is as smart as all of us together." With collaboration, we see that the answers to many of the motivational challenges students face reside within a school.

EXHIBIT 3.1

Strategies for Expanding Time for Collaboration

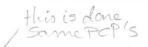

[handwritten: this is done, same PCP's]

- Ask staff to identify with whom and when they need to collaborate and redesign the master schedule to accommodate faculty's needs for time in which to collaborate on planning, teaching, and reflection.

- Hire permanent substitutes to rotate through classrooms to periodically free teachers to attend meetings during the day rather than before or after school. *[handwritten: expensive –]*

- Institute a community service component in the curriculum; teachers meet while students are out in the community (for example, Thursday afternoons). *[handwritten: not possible, unpractical]*

- Schedule "specials" (for example, art and music), clubs, and tutorials during the same time blocks so that teachers have one or two hours a day to collaborate. *[handwritten: need certificate person in charge]*

- Engage parents, family members, and community members in planning and conducting half-day or full-day exploratory sessions that teach literacy skills in motivating ways (for example, creating recipes for a cookbook in a gourmet cooking session, writing a script for a puppet theater, publishing an emergency CPR manual in a class in emergency medicine), theater, or other experiential programs. *[handwritten: not practical for us]*

- Partner with colleges and universities to have their faculty teach in your school or offer distance learning lessons, demonstrations, and on-campus experiences to free up school personnel.

- Rearrange the school day to include a fifty- to sixty-minute block of time before or after school for collaborative meeting or planning.

- Arrange to meet after school, after students leave and before faculty members leave. When teachers add forty-five minutes to one day a week—and leave earlier on another day of their choice as compensation—they have a nice block of time to work together.

Source: Villa and Thousand, 1995, p. 67.

Additional ideas for finding time:

EXHIBIT 3.2

Sample Approach for Banking Time

Some schools wish to "bank" time. They extend the instructional minutes taught during four of the five weekly school days to shorten the instructional minutes taught during one school day. This provides time for staff to meet during the shortened instruction day to collaborate on enhancing student learning. Following is an example of how one school decided to accomplish this.

Raya Elementary School

Raya Elementary staff members wanted to create time to collaborate on improving teaching practices and enhancing student learning. After much discussion, the staff decided to bank instructional time, opting for four longer instructional days so that they could shorten one day of the week (Wednesday). On Wednesdays the students would go home at 1:10 P.M. instead of at 3:00 P.M., allowing teachers to meet from 1:15 to 3:00 P.M.

Staff used the first three Wednesdays of the month for grade-level collaboration meetings and the last Wednesday for a schoolwide collaboration meeting. Raya Elementary was able to devote thirty-seven Wednesdays during the school year to grade-level and schoolwide collaboration. To ensure that the school met instructional minute requirements for the school year, staff devised the following schedules for primary (K–3) and intermediate students (grades 4 through 6):

	Primary	Intermediate
Nonstaggered days	8 × 265 minutes = 2,210 minutes	5 × 265 minutes = 1,325 minutes
Regular days	131 × 325 minutes = 42,575 minutes	134 × 325 minutes = 43,550 minutes
Shortened days	37 × 225 minutes = 8,325 minutes	37 × 225 minutes = 8,325 minutes
Minimum days	4 × 170 minutes = 680 minutes	4 × 220 minutes = 800 minutes
	Total = 53,700 minutes	Total = 54,000 minutes

Grade-level weekly meetings focused on already developed lessons for enhancing student motivation and learning and assessments for clarifying standards that needed to be retaught. Staff used schoolwide monthly meetings to share individual grades' accomplishments and challenges, expand on strategies that would help to implement powerful teaching and learning in all classrooms, and assess to what degree the school was accomplishing its schoolwide goals.

A special thank you to Pablo Fiene for this sample approach to banking time.

Notes: *Hard for our families to work with this ? buses?*

EXHIBIT 3.3
Sample Peer Observation Schedule

just one grade level teacher

Time Frame	Peer Observation Approach	Participants
Week One: Fifteen minutes	Host partner shares lesson design.	All faculty
Week One: Thirty minutes	Visiting partner observes host partner using partnership guide or data in a day rubric.	All faculty
Week One: Ten minutes (minimum)	Debrief during planning period (with compensation time)	All faculty
Week One: Five minutes	Both partners set a goal (goal setting)	All faculty
Week Two: Cycle repeats with partners exchanging roles.	Cycle repeats.	All faculty

Blank Peer Observation Schedule

Time Frame	Peer Observation Approach	Participants

EXHIBIT 3.4

Data in a Day: Inclusion (Respect and Connectedness)

	Yes, Obvious	Yes, but	Not Seen This Visit	Ideas
Routines and rituals are present that contribute to respectful learning (e.g. ground rules, cooperative learning).				
Students comfortably and respectfully interact with each other.				
Students comfortably and respectfully interact with teacher (e.g. students share their perspectives).				
Teacher treats all students respectfully and fairly.				

General Information/Comments

EXHIBIT 3.5

Data in a Day: Attitude (Choice and Personal or Cultural Relevance)

	Ideas	Not Seen This Visit	Yes, but	Yes, Obvious
Classes are taught with students' experiences, concerns or interests in mind.				
Students make choices related to learning that include experiences, values, needs and strengths.				
Students are able to voice their opinions.				
Teacher varies how students learn (discussion, music, film, personal interaction).				

General Information/Comments

EXHIBIT 3.6

Data in a Day: Meaning (Challenge and Engagement)

	Yes, Obvious	Yes, but	Not Seen This Visit	Ideas
Students actively participate in challenging ways (e.g. engaging in investigations, projects, art, simulations, case study).				
Teacher asks questions that go beyond facts and encourages students to learn from different points of view.				
Teacher helps students recall what they know and build on it.				
Teacher respectfully encourages high quality responses.				

General Information/Comments

EXHIBIT 3.7

Data in a Day: Competence (Authenticity and Effectiveness)

	Yes, Obvious	Yes, but	Not Seen This Visit	Ideas
Teacher shares or develops with students clear criteria for success (e.g. rubrics, personal conferences).				
Grading policies are fair to all students (e.g. students can learn from mistakes and the grades reflect what students know and can do).				
There are performances and demonstrations with real-world connections.				
Assessment includes student values (e.g. students self-assess there are multiple ways to demonstrate learning).				

General Information/Comments

EXHIBIT 3.8

Profile of an Effective Organizational Team

(The categories as well as the items for consideration are an integration of research on effective teams and themes or needs for creating change in institutions. Please rate your responses in terms of lowest and highest priorities (1 = low; 5 = high).

General Direction of the Team

	Low	Middle	High	Examples
1. The team has a shared vision and mission that focuses on students and highly motivating instructional practice.	1 2	3 4	5	_____
2. The team develops a manageable work plan with clear goals.	1 2	3 4	5	_____
3. The team focuses on activities that have a significant impact on all students.	1 2	3 4	5	_____
4. The team participates in the development and implementation of the schoolwide plan.	1 2	3 4	5	_____
5. The team ensures that the diversity elements of the schoolwide plan are substantive and well integrated.	1 2	3 4	5	_____

Meetings

	Low	Middle	High	Examples
1. The team meets at least once a month.	1 2	3 4	5	_____
2. Team meetings are scheduled in advance, and participants are notified of meeting times.	1 2	3 4	5	_____
3. Team members have an opportunity to contribute to the formation of the agenda.	1 2	3 4	5	_____
4. Team members attend regularly.	1 2	3 4	5	_____
5. Minutes are kept of all meetings and are made available to key constituencies when appropriate.	1 2	3 4	5	_____
6. Team members conduct work as needed between meetings, with the necessary support to make professional decisions that effectively and efficiently respond to the needs of their school.	1 2	3 4	5	_____

Ability to Work as a Team

	Low		Middle		High	Examples
1. Team members effectively communicate with each other.	1	2	3	4	5	_____
2. Team members use consensus decision-making skills, and all members fully participate in discussions as well as decisions.	1	2	3	4	5	_____
3. The team uses members' skills and areas of expertise.	1	2	3	4	5	_____
4. Team members support each other in fulfilling responsibilities.	1	2	3	4	5	_____
5. Team members resolve conflicts and problems effectively.	1	2	3	4	5	_____
6. The team works to ensure that all members feel included and valued.	1	2	3	4	5	_____
7. The team regularly assesses itself.	1	2	3	4	5	_____

Leadership

	Low		Middle		High	Examples
1. The leader works with team members to clarify respective roles and responsibilities.	1	2	3	4	5	_____
2. The leader works collaboratively with all team members.	1	2	3	4	5	_____
3. The leader acts as a facilitative leader in team decision making.	1	2	3	4	5	_____
4. The leader ensures that all team members have the timely information they need to make decisions.	1	2	3	4	5	_____
5. Members of the team share leadership and responsibility for the team's work.	1	2	3	4	5	_____
6. The leader encourages diversity of opinions and ideas.	1	2	3	4	5	_____
7. The leader encourages creativity and risk taking.	1	2	3	4	5	_____

External Communication

	Low		Middle		High	Examples
1. The team seeks input from school staff, administrative personnel, students, community members, and other constituencies in an equitable manner.	1	2	3	4	5	_____
2. The team effectively communicates with all professional development initiatives about relevant issues.	1	2	3	4	5	_____
3. The team fully informs school constituencies of its activities and outcomes.	1	2	3	4	5	_____
4. The team uses an external as well as an internal communication plan. (External refers to the communities at large, and internal refers to the community within the institution.)	1	2	3	4	5	_____

Source: Adapted from Hirsh (n.d.)

Use this space to note your priorities:

EXHIBIT 3.9

Grade-Level Agenda

Facilitator: _____Timekeeper: _____

Reporter: _____Recorder: _____

I. Introduction (approximately five minutes)
Follow up with individuals on agreed-upon goals from the last meeting or general sharing.

II. Professional Development or Collaborative Work (twenty-five minutes)
Do grade-level or thematic lesson planning that addresses standards or grade-level assessment for student learning related to standards; plan reteaching opportunities.

III. Next Steps (five minutes)
Documentation: complete individual and group follow-through goals.

IV. Grade-Level Concerns or Upcoming Events (fifteen minutes)

V. Plan Agenda for Following Meeting (ten minutes)
Documentation: write a brief summary of the meeting to share with the principal for schoolwide communication.

Reflection on meeting: How are we doing with our norms and goals?

Signatures of Meeting Attendees:

_____

(Sample) Grade-Level Meeting Norms
We agree to maintain an atmosphere of mutual respect.
We agree to maintain structure in our meetings.
We agree to be on time and prepared with all necessary materials (including documents that demonstrate follow-through on last week's agreements).
We agree to participate by sharing ideas.
We agree to participate by sharing concerns as problems that can be solved.
We agree to reach decisions by consensus after hearing all opinions.

Comments/Feedback from Principal:

78 Motivation Matters

EXHIBIT 3.10
Examining Student Work

Level of Student Work	Next Steps	Goals
Advanced		
Proficient		
Partially proficient		
Students with special needs		

EXHIBIT 3.11

Meeting Summary Sheet

Grade level, department, or core: _____

Members present: _____

Date:_____

Topic or focus of grade-level, department, or core work:

_____

_____

_____

Summary of discussion:

_____

_____

_____

Lessons or units planned:

_____

_____

_____

Lessons to be taught between today and the next meeting:

_____

_____

_____

Student work to bring to the next meeting:

_____

_____

_____

Next meeting:_____

EXHIBIT 3.12

Sample Outcomes Using the Meeting Summary Sheet

Date: *Jan. 15, 2003*

Topic or focus of grade-level, department, or core work:
Using principles of motivation to strengthen students basic awareness of standards, enhancing proficiency with multiple choice formats.

Summary of discussion:
The fourth-grade team reviewed its accomplishments to date. It also identified two ongoing challenges: using standards to focus learning and helping students to be more aware of how to use multiple-choice formats.

Lessons or units planned:
* *Develop and share teacher-made assessments for math standards.*
* *Review language arts standards with students (using the report card as an initial guide). Have a different student (or pair of students) write a different standard on a sentence strips. In fact, have students create two sentence strips for each language arts standard—one to signify the definition of the standard and one to signify an original example/application of the standard. Color-code the two sentence strips, e.g. yellow for the standard and green for an example/application of the standard.*
* *Visit Arlene's room to observe the "standards on sentence strips" process as she tries it out with her students. (Use the grade-level planning period prior to the visit to collectively develop the sample approach—using the motivational framework)*
* *Begin "post office," i.e. a weekly round-robin between classes in which each class develops, for another class, a quiz question based on a standard that has been identified as needing reinforcement—based on the monthly language arts unit assessment. Friday mornings, each class posts the question they have developed (in multiple choice format) on the door of a designated classroom. Friday afternoons, each class returns their response to the class that authored the question and that class determines whether the answer is correct. Chart the number of correct responses.*

Lessons to be taught between today and the next meeting:
* *Continue science investigations.*
* *Review concepts from science curriculum to prepare students for a study trip to the Discovery Museum.*
* *All teachers are in same lesson in unit three of the language arts curriculum and will continue at a similar pace.*

Student work to bring to the next meeting:
Unit Three Language Arts Assessment Results

Next meeting:
* *Share teacher-made assessments for math standards.*
* *Create an implementation timeline for math assessments.*
* *Examine student work from Unit Three Language Arts Assessment.*
* *Identify standards that need to be retaught.*
* *Design a motivating approach to reteach language arts standards with which students still struggle.*

Chapter 4

Using Data to Strengthen Motivation and Learning

THIS CHAPTER PROVIDES approaches to two kinds of data: (1) original data related to student motivation and learning, as well as professional development benchmarks; and (2) data from standardized tests. With respect to student motivation and learning, original data includes processes mentioned in other chapters, such as the lesson-study process (Chapter Three, Activity Three) and insights from peer coaching (Chapter Three, Activity Two). This chapter builds on that approach so that teachers can create cohesive process-folios to assess teaching over time, in ways that include multiple strategies for learning from practice.

This chapter also features two processes about which schools have expressed particular interest. They require some initial set-up work to help faculty feel comfortable, because they involve asking teachers to open their classroom doors to strangers. These processes heighten consciousness about and sharpen the focus on daily instruction.

One process, data in a day, was originally developed at Northwest Regional Educational Laboratory (www.nwrel.org). As a one-day collaborative action-research experience, it allows several teams of teachers, community members, and students to visit classrooms to take a "snapshot" of teaching and learning. They look for ways in which the school is achieving the motivational ideals to which it aspires. The approach to data in a day offered in this book includes rubrics that are anchored in research on motivation and learning.

This chapter also outlines administrative walk-throughs, an approach in which the principal or an administrative team makes short unscheduled classroom visits on a regular basis. Although walk-throughs serve several purposes, a key attribute is that they strengthen the principal's ability to serve as an active and informed advocate of inspired teaching.

Action research is another means to collect original data. This chapter illustrates a way that faculty can collect and analyze data from classroom practice. But it also includes approaches to use with existing data, such as data from standardized tests, to clarify which content standards students seem to be learning and which ones require additional emphasis. This includes an approach to record keeping so that teacher teams can collaborate for the purposes of reteaching and drawing on each other's professional strengths. In addition, the chapter includes benchmarks for school improvement that may seem peripheral but are key aspects that contribute to or reflect on motivating learning. These include staff development and parent and family involvement.

Finally, artifacts and insights from professional demonstrations, such as the poster-conference activity in this chapter, provide additional clues for how a school is taking action and developing insights related to those actions. Poster conferences provide a school with a way to creatively highlight practices they have found most supportive of student motivation.

Professional Process-Folios

Activity One: Professional Process-Folios

Purpose   To organize, examine, and communicate lessons and teaching practices that support student motivation and learning

Participants   Teachers working individually and in pairs

Time   Ongoing

Materials   Exhibit 4.1 (process-folio case), Exhibit 4.2 (sample lesson), and Exhibit 4.3 (overall organization) (pp. 96–99)

Process   Explain that the purpose of a process-folio is to develop, organize, and examine unit plans, lesson plans, assessments of student learning, and resources in a manner that supports the schoolwide goal of enhancing student motivation and learning.

Ask participants to work with a partner to identify how a useful process-folio might be organized. See Exhibit 4.3 (p. 99).

Create a time line for implementing the various process-folio chapters. Schedule an individual meeting with an instructional leader (typically a school administrator) to review process-folio goals and identify forms of support for follow-through. (*Note:* Although this process is of value to all teachers, it is especially useful to new teachers. When teacher-mentors work alongside a protégé, the process contributes to the professional development of both participants.)

Walk-Throughs

Picture this scene: It is 9:00 A.M., and with her phone ringing, Suzanne Gabriel, principal of Audre Lorde Middle School, hurries to meet her assistant principal and two counselors. As on all Mondays, they clarify which classrooms they will be visiting throughout the week. With prior input and consent from teachers, the school is using a five-minute walk-through process to further its vision of motivation and learning among diverse students.

The approach includes visits to a variety of classrooms three times a week by each of the four team members. With each member of the walk-through team visiting three classrooms on Monday, Tuesday, and Thursday, they will be able to provide insights based on forty-eight classroom visits at the monthly staff meeting.

Teachers appreciate the anonymous but concrete feedback about teaching and learning. They believe that this heightens awareness of the ways in which their teaching is loyal to their schoolwide emphasis on highly motivating instruction. Administrators appreciate the ways in which they are able to develop their knowledge about curriculum and instruction and serve as well-informed instructional leaders. As a complement to other motivationally anchored schoolwide practices, walk-throughs have played a vital role in Audre Lorde Middle School's success.

Activity Two: Five-Minute Walk-Throughs by Instructional Leaders

Purpose   To determine, as a faculty, how five-minute regular visits to classrooms by instructional leaders can contribute to the vitality of a school

Participants   Small groups of five or six teachers for carousel graffiti

Time   Thirty minutes

Materials   Article "How Walk-Throughs Open Doors" by Margery B. Ginsberg and Damon Murphy (Appendix A)

Process

Step one: Distribute the walk-through agenda developed using the motivational framework (Exhibit 4.4, p. 100). Facilitate a KWL process to answer the questions: What do I know (K)? What do I want to know (W)? What have I learned (L)?

Step two: Distribute the article "How Walk-Throughs Open Doors." Ask participants to read the article, noting ideas related to the W or "What I want to know" list.

Step three: Facilitate a carousel graffiti activity (see Chapter Two, Activity Three) to address the following questions:

- How might a walk-through process contribute to our school's approach to renewal?

- What are some of the reasons we might want to do periodic walk-through visits?

- What do we want to include in our walk-through guide? (See sample guide in Exhibit 4.5, p. 101.)

- What kind of faculty feedback would be respectful and useful?

- What logistics should we consider in planning walk-throughs (for example, which rooms, when, how often).

- What other data might we gather and analyze to complement insights from walk-through visits?

- How can we create a positive experience for participants?

The walk-through summary form in Exhibit 4.6 (p. 103) provides a concise tool for summarizing results from Exhibit 4.5. It also helps to identify trends across classrooms.

Further information about walk-throughs is available in Ginsberg and Wlodkowski (2000) and Ginsberg (2001).

Data in a Day

In the high-poverty schools in which I work, members of the school community scrutinize conventional data based on standardized tests, promotion and retention rates, attendance records, and so forth. But they realize that state or district data do not directly lead to an understanding of how teaching and learning occurs throughout an entire school nor, in particular, to a dialogue about how to create the conditions in classrooms that contribute to intrinsic motivation and substantive learning among diverse student groups. School-improvement dialogue based solely on an analysis of conventional forms of data can circumvent one of the foremost challenges facing educators: how to support students' intrinsic motivation, their value for and interest in learning, given the heterogeneity of experiences, beliefs, and modes of learning in contemporary classrooms.

Data in a day can help a school engage in focused dialogue about teaching and learning as well as create a schoolwide willingness to experiment. In addition, it jump-starts commitment to school renewal when enthusiasm plateaus. And when students share their perspectives, even if it is to a high school faculty of 130 teachers, you can hear a pin drop. That in itself serves as a valuable reminder that even when philosophies differ and practices fail, learning can unite.

Activity Three: Data in a Day

Purpose To take a snapshot of how teaching and learning look throughout an entire school in a single day, to engage parents and students as partners in ongoing school renewal

Participants School community in groups of five to six

Time One hour to introduce the process

Format Carousel graffiti

Materials Article "By the Numbers" by Margery B. Ginsberg (Appendix B), handout of Exhibit 4.7 (p. 104).

Process Members of the planning team that coordinates the process review the article on data in a day from the Journal of Staff Development and the information in Exhibit 4.7 to customize the approach to their school.

Data in a day promotes the school renewal attributes that successful schools share. These include sincere engagement of students, parents, community members, and district-level personnel in continuous renewal; job-embedded learning with a clear focus on teaching and learning; and in some districts (such as Spring Branch, Texas; Alum Rock, California; and Albany, New York) assertive critical questioning about assumptions related to effort and reward as driving forces in academic achievement among diverse learners. One of data in a day's greatest virtues is that teachers are able to see for themselves clear examples of classroom practices that invite student engagement across demographic groups, with a learning environment that is culturally respectful and motivationally significant.

As an educational tool, data in a day helps to dispel myths about motivational deficits within student groups. In doing so this process can lead to a rich dialogue about the destructiveness of blame and about practices such as labeling and "fixing" students through programs that pull students out of class for additional help. Perhaps most of all, data in a day encourages the understanding of the ways in which intrinsic motivation resides in all people and how to support it across all racial, ethnic, and cultural groups. When students (whether children or adults) can see that what they are learning makes sense and is important according to their values and perspectives, intrinsic motivation surfaces like a cork rising through water (Ginsberg and Wlodkowski, 2000). Data in a day can help to create those environments—for teachers as well as students.

Activity Four: Action Research

Purpose   To collect and analyze data focusing on a school renewal topic articulated in the school-improvement plan, in order to improve individual, team, or schoolwide performance

Participants   Teams of educators at a school site

Time   Regularly scheduled daily and weekly meetings

Format   Discussion and data collection

Materials   Handouts about action-research approach (Exhibits 4.8 and 4.9, pp. 105–108)

Process   Teams of educators at a school site decide on an essential question related to an ongoing challenge in their classroom or to the schoolwide plan. They will collect and analyze related data and use insights to inform new types of action.

   Step one: Select a focus. This includes (1) determining what you want to investigate, (2) developing a question about the area you have chosen, and (3) establishing a plan to investigate the question based on a hypothesis. A good initial exercise to elicit a question is a five-minute written reflection about something that the individual or team cares about but hasn't yet been able to figure out.

   Step two: Collect data. Once you have identified a research question and agreed on an investigative approach, you are ready to collect the information (data) to guide insights related to your research question.

   Step three: Analyze and interpret the data. Based on your analysis of the data, share your findings: describe the data; summarize them; and identify patterns or themes among them. Discuss insights with your colleagues to enhance your understanding, and use insights or decisions to develop a new hypothesis to explore.

   Step four: Elaborate on the action-research process. Use your analysis and conclusions to elaborate on previous actions regarding instructional or organizational practices.

Activity Five: Using Data to Inform the Implementation of School Renewal Goals

Purpose   Developing goals and collecting related data is a key aspect of helping a school stay committed to systematic and sustained change. The following renewal goals and forms of data can guide a school as it engages in renewal based on motivationally anchored teaching and learning.

Participants   Teachers, administrators, and parents

Time   Full day prior to school beginning, followed by weekly leadership team meetings, weekly grade-level meetings, and monthly faculty meetings

Format   Retreat and evaluation-team meetings

Materials Measurement tools for student academic achievement (test scores from standardized and teacher-made assessments, grades, writing portfolios); measurement tools for parent-involvement activities (attendance rosters, teacher phone-log contacts, classroom visits); measurement tools for staff development activities (ongoing review of lessons teachers submit to schoolwide process-folios of motivating approaches to teaching various standards, peer-coaching artifacts and reflections, sample lesson-study artifacts such as the quality of warm and cool feedback from video or real-time sharing of teaching, and summaries of weekly team planning)

Process Ideally, at an annual retreat before the school year begins, school staff agree upon the school renewal goals for the academic year. After this meeting the instructional leadership cadre or a school-based evaluation team comprising teachers (one from each grade level), parents, and administrators conducts an ongoing evaluation to measure the degree to which the school is meeting its school renewal goals.

After school staff has reviewed and agreed on its renewal goals, the school-based evaluation team meets to decide on ways to measure achievement of the renewal goals, data to collect, responsibilities to be shared, and the time line that the team will follow. Next, the team meets weekly to evaluate ongoing accomplishment of school renewal goals and to provide insight into what steps staff needs to take to ensure schoolwide progress. The team shares this information during weekly grade-level meetings and monthly schoolwide meetings, such as staff meetings, to share and exchange insights on school renewal goal accomplishments. The following case study illustrates the process.

• • •

Rubiner Elementary School

After conducting a comprehensive needs assessment, the staff at Rubiner has identified five goals to achieve in its schoolwide reform effort (the first two are shared throughout the district; the last three are specific to Rubiner Elementary):

Goal one: Eighty percent of Rubiner Elementary students who attended the school for three or more consecutive years will meet or exceed state standards in reading, language arts, computational skills, and application of mathematical concepts.

Goal two: Seventy-five percent of students who attended Rubiner for at least one year but less than three full consecutive years will meet or exceed state standards in reading, language arts, spelling, computational skills, and application of mathematical concepts.

Goal three: *Sixty percent of students who attended Rubiner for less than one year will meet or exceed state standards in reading, language arts, spelling, computational skills, and application of mathematical concepts.*

Goal four: *Eighty percent of instructional staff will demonstrate knowledge of effective instructional strategies and will apply the four conditions of the motivational framework to all instruction.*

Goal five: *Rubiner families will develop a sense of connectedness to the school and participate more in their children's education.*

[handwritten margin note: *note the will*]

[handwritten note: *if we could make them do that*]

After the staff agreed on the five school renewal goals, school principal Sylvia de la Cruz felt strongly that the school would need to use goals as a guide throughout the year. To do this an ongoing assessment of accomplishments would be necessary. However, because of daily demands on classroom teachers, the principal suggested at the faculty meeting that the school create a school-based evaluation team made up of the principal and one teacher representative from each grade level. The purpose of the team would be to create indicators of success for each renewal goal and to use indicators to decide on data to collect; divide responsibilities among team members; and develop a time line that the team, in collaboration with the school, would maintain as a priority. The team would also be responsible for providing regular updates of its activities as well as information on the extent to which Rubiner was achieving its goals. It would provide these updates through the regularly scheduled weekly grade-level meetings, schoolwide staff meetings, and a monthly evaluation-team bulletin.

• • •

When the team first met, it created the matrix shown in Exhibit 4.10 (p. 109). To measure each professional development goal, the cadre developed benchmarks. Following are examples of the team's agreed-upon benchmarks for measuring progress toward Goal Four:

1. Eighty percent of grade-level team members will devise jointly and apply a minimum of four motivational framework grade-level weekly lesson plans in their classrooms during the school year.

    • To assess this goal, each teacher will submit grade-level lesson plans and self-report on the development and implementation of the lessons. (Exhibit 4.11, p. 111 provides the rubric that Rubiner teachers created to assess the clarity of their plans, each of which was contributed to the schoolwide process-folio of sample motivating, standards-based lessons.)

2. Eighty percent of Rubiner teachers will demonstrate comfort in using the motivational framework in their classrooms and apply it in their grade-level language arts curriculum.

   • To assess this goal, each teacher will participate in classroom observations, review of lesson designs, or video demonstrations.

3. Eighty percent of Rubiner teachers will establish a minimum of one professional learning goal and demonstrate progress on achieving that goal.

   • To assess this goal, each teacher will establish a professional learning goal for him- or herself and report monthly on his or her efforts to pursue the learning objective. Examples of such learning could include action research based on helping a low-performing student to become an intellectual leader, creating a student project related to the learning area, or hosting a brown-bag lunch to share and apply articles.

4. By the end of the school year, 75 percent of the teachers will report that they believe that school goals align with professional development at Rubiner Elementary.

   • Teachers will self-report semiannually, and yearly teacher interviews will track this goal.

To measure parent involvement, the evaluation team developed measurable benchmarks. Following are examples of the team's benchmarks for measuring progress toward goal five:

1. Fifty percent of Rubiner Elementary parents will participate in ongoing school activities as follows:

   • Open house, back to school night, any schoolwide functions

   • Parent literacy nights

   • Parent-teacher interactions and communications (journal, parent-teacher phone calls, parent-teacher meetings, and so on)

   • Parent volunteers: service day, parent volunteer in classrooms, leading before- and after-school activities

   • Parent learning opportunities: English as a second language, parents helping students with homework (homework club), reading club, and so on

2. Sixty percent of Rubiner families will be actively involved in their child's learning and work with the school to improve their child's success.

3. Teachers will contact 75 percent of their students' families, at least three times a year (once a trimester) by telephone or letter.

-   The school will assess parent involvement goals in the following ways:

-   Staff will systematically track parent attendance at every event held at Rubiner Elementary. Every teacher, group leader, and event planner will provide a means to ensure that parents sign in for the event. All parent sign-in lists will be given to the evaluator each month for schoolwide tallies and analysis for demographic equity.

-   Teachers will complete monthly reports on all teacher contact with parents. Each teacher will submit the monthly reports to the school evaluation team, which will then create schoolwide tallies and summarize results.

-   Each teacher will provide opportunities for parents to be involved in their child's education, either through a weekly homework folder, joint parent-child learning projects, or other means. Each month teachers will assess the extent to which parents participated in activities. They will report their analysis to the school evaluation team, which will then compile schoolwide data.

After developing benchmarks, the Rubiner team created a time line for the year (Exhibit 4.12, p. 112). The team scheduled most of the foundational work to be done in August and September.

Surveys and Other Tools

The surveys and tools provided in this section can help schools evaluate their renewal goals based on the motivational framework. Embedded within each survey are indicators of the four motivational conditions. The first two surveys (Exhibits 4.13 and 4.14, pp. 114 and 115) are addressed to teachers.

Alongside lesson plans and classroom observations, the information from these surveys can help measure the degree to which instructional staff is implementing the four conditions of the motivational framework.

A monthly report on professional development activities can help a focus on its commitments and assess progress. The monthly reporting tool in Exhibit 4.15 (p. 116) can be used for updating members of the school community at staff and faculty meetings and meetings with the broader community.

Regularly conducted surveys help a school assess the extent to which instructional staff is implementing motivating, standards-based instructional strategies. To assess the influence of a schoolwide focus on motivation and learning from students' perspectives, the survey in Exhibit 4.16 (p. 118) may be useful.

The survey is administered by the school site evaluation team by grade level (grades 3 to 6 in elementary schools), and by subject (reading, math, computers, and science) to compare subject areas and grades. The comparisons can lead to helpful insights. Sample survey results can be found in Exhibit 4.17 (p. 119).

To measure the extent to which families are developing a sense of connectedness to the school and their children's education, the school evaluation team may find the following tools helpful: the parent survey (Exhibit 4.18, p. 120), the parent-teacher contact log (Exhibit 4.19, p. 121), and the parent involvement log (Exhibit 4.20, p. 122).

To ensure feedback from all families and assess similarities and differences among various linguistic, ethnic, and cultural groups, surveys need to be translated into the families' primary language.

Once filled out, these surveys and logs help a school evaluation team to measure the extent to which all families feel connected to the school's educational process.

Whereas surveys require quite a bit of attention to administer, the contacts that teachers record in the parent-teacher contact log provide immediate feedback to the school community. Schools generally find this simple tool invaluable.

Academic Organizer

The following tools can help school teams collect on the primary renewal goal, student learning. They provide a form of visual clarity that can contribute to a dialogue about the topic. This often leads to more creative approaches to reteaching standards with which students continue to struggle. In several schools teachers use these tools to analyze weekly assessment results in various academic subjects during their grade-level meetings. If a school agrees, planning teams may find it useful to share their results with the school evaluation team so that the school as a whole can identify patterns and trends.

One useful tool is the setting of standards and assigning a criterion score for each. Exhibit 4.21 (p. 124) gives an example, using a lesson in measurement and geometry.

Note: Several exhibits are based on work that was facilitated by Dr. Katherine Armstrong in concert with the Cabrillo Leadership Team at Cabrillo Elementary School in Fremont, California. A special note of gratitude to Dr. Armstrong and Cabrillo Elementary School.

Standardized Tests

The best kinds of tests resemble real learning tasks that have instructional value. They also require complex and challenging mental processes, often acknowledging more than one approach or right answer. Perhaps most importantly, good tests are meaningful to students. When tests are meaningful, when topics really matter to students (and are even a bit playful), students lose fear and engage their multiple talents in even the most challenging processes (Wlodkowski and Ginsberg, 1995). Although standardized tests rarely share these attributes, they provide information that is used to make judgments about students, often throughout life. Under the right circumstances, schools can prepare students for standardized tests and use them to enhance motivation and learning. The following activity exemplifies how to anchor test preparation in the motivational framework.

Activity Six: Helping Students Prepare for State Tests

Purpose   To use preparation for standardized tests as a means to contribute to individual, team, and schoolwide motivation and performance

Participants   Educators

Time   One-half hour or as needed at weekly grade-level or department meetings

Format   Individual reading and team discussion

Materials   Handout of Exhibit 4.22 (p. 125)

Process   Schoolwide teams of educators challenge themselves to find spirited ways to strengthen student motivation and skills related to showing how much students already know when they take standardized tests.

Review the schoolwide communication agreement, with an emphasis on maintaining a hopeful orientation, for example, posing challenges as problems that can be solved. Ask teams to brainstorm what has helped them to prepare students to do well on the state test.

Distribute the case study (Exhibit 4.22) to stimulate memory and contribute additional ideas. Ask team members to read the case and add to their brainstorming list any way they think might further their students' success.

Ask for two volunteer scribes to chart on newsprint what team representatives collectively report. Next, ask for a representative from each team to come to the front of the room with representatives from other teams. Tell them you would like for them to share their team's ideas in a round-robin manner. Representatives form a line at the front of the room, sharing only one idea at a time in a rotating fashion until they have no more ideas to share. Scribes capture ideas on newsprint. Transcribe and distribute these schoolwide to stimulate the creation of team-specific agreements that can contribute to students' confidence, skill, and success in taking tests.

Activity Seven: Developing a Statement of Purpose for a Schoolwide Process-Folio

Purpose   To develop a shared sense of purpose to guide the development of a school process-folio

Participants   School staff

Time   One hour

Materials   Handout of Exhibit 4.23 (p. 126)

Process   Explain that a process-folio goes beyond the traditional portfolio, which typically contains select examples of highly polished work. A process-folio helps document and reflect on challenges and emerging understandings over time (Wlodkowski and Ginsberg, 1995). Ask participants to share what comes to mind when they think of a school process-folio. Ask what would help a schoolwide process-folio to be a useful process as opposed to just another task.

Explain that a statement of purpose is necessary to guide the process of process-folio development and use. To use time as efficiently as possible, ask staff to review the draft statement of purpose in Exhibit 4.23 as a starting point. Ask staff to underline what they like, change or delete what they don't like, and add whatever is necessary from their perspective. Post results on a "reading wall" and work together to synthesize comments to create a customized statement of purpose.

Activity Eight: Developing an Outline for a School Process-folio

Purpose   To develop an outline and process through which to organize, unify, analyze, and further develop school goals and accomplishments

Participants   Instructional leadership cadre

Time   Initially, one hour

Materials   Handout of Exhibit 4.24 (p. 126)

Process   Read through Exhibit 4.24 to get an idea of what a school process-folio might contain. Customize the outline based on an agreed-upon purpose. Develop a time line that includes (1) organizing documents, (2) reviewing the portfolio with school staff, (3) reflecting with colleagues on accomplishments and challenges, and (4) creating personal and schoolwide goals.

The goal of this activity is to produce a process-folio that is an authentic part of the school renewal process, as opposed to an isolated and cumbersome accountability task.

Assign a time limit to each previously mentioned item. Remind the planning team that this is a draft for whole-school review and feedback. A useful resource is *The School Portfolio: A Comprehensive Framework for School Improvement* by Victoria Bernhardt (1999). In addition, the Maine Department of Education (207-624-6629), with input from Comprehensive School Reform Demonstration sites throughout the state, has developed helpful guidelines for building and reporting on CSRD activities.

Poster Conference

A *poster conference* is an interactive method for sharing exhibitions, ideas, and questions. It provides an opportunity for leadership cadre members to engage in dialogue with each other, central office staff, school board members, and key members of the community about creatively displayed topics.

The team (or teams of teachers throughout a school) prepares a poster, a display, or a demonstration that represents its focus and accomplishments. Poster conferences have included sample lesson designs using the motivational framework with photographs of the learning process labeled with principles of motivation; creative displays of student work and of the four conditions of the motivational framework that supported their success; strategies that correspond to the framework with visual aids to demonstrate how they work; and computer simulations, time lines, or cognitive maps that show how team members' initiative evolved and was integrated into their school-improvement plan.

A reflection sheet for each display of the cadre's posters can provide evidence from observers of their increased knowledge of how to create highly motivating classroom instruction, design inquiry-based projects for the school, provide school-improvement processes that matter, create strong collaborative teams focused on improving student learning, examine student work in order to transform historically low-achieving students to intellectual leaders, and develop faculty institutes that invite an ongoing dialogue about cultural diversity and student achievement. When each exhibit provides a one-page summary, visitors have something to help them recall their learning, and the school has contributions to its process-folio that includes insights and best practices gained from the initiative.

Activity Nine: Poster Conferences

Purpose   To imaginatively create displays that illuminate aspects of a school-based or districtwide renewal initiative based on highly motivating teaching and learning for all students

Participants   Leadership cadre(s) or grade-level or department teams throughout a school

Time   2.5 hours

Format   Interactive small group(s)

Materials   Plenty of space for displays and dialogue, lunch, handout of Exhibit 4.25 (p. 127)

Process   This is an opportunity for participants to collaboratively plan a poster conference to represent yearlong actions, learning, and accomplishments. As a group, review the handout of Exhibit 4.25 and explain that the group will begin planning by brainstorming ideas for a poster conference using the carousel graffiti process outlined in Chapter Two, Activity Three. Recommended questions for carousel graffiti or brainstorming follow:

- What might be the goals of a poster conference?

- What topics might we present at different poster conference displays?

- What might a display look like? (For example, outline an approach; create a display of pictures and photographs showing an idea in action; videotape a teacher showing the motivational framework in action; interview students about their learning experiences; demonstrate how a school found time for job-embedded learning and other forms of adult collaboration; develop a scrapbook.)

- How could a poster conference be a stepping-stone to other forms of adult learning?

- What kinds of logistics might you recommend? (For example, coordination of teams, action plans from each team, outline of what posters might look like, room for a district-level display, one-page summary for visitors about each display, publicity before and after the event, photography, food, and a portfolio based on the conference.)

Summary

As most educators realize, the pressure for higher standards and greater measures of accountability are often inspired as much by political self-interest as by a genuine concern for schools and the children and communities to which they belong. Nonetheless, across the nation innumerable sincere and inspiring schools serve as examples of what it takes to keep the dream of strong public education alive. When we look closely at what adults are learning and doing, no matter how they name it, we consistently see principles of intrinsic motivation at work.

EXHIBIT 4.1

Benally Elementary School

At Benally Elementary School, the second-grade-level team decided to jointly develop a lesson process-folio to assist them in implementing the motivational framework in a more comprehensive manner. On Monday after school, the team decided that for the next week they would jointly develop five lessons that addressed word analysis, specifically vocabulary development and spelling. Initially, they outlined the lessons to be taught using the following form:

Lesson Plan Outline: Month:

Date	Topic	Motivational Framework Strategies	Assessment	Standards

One-day Sample Lesson Plan Outline: Month:

Date	Topic	Motivational Framework Strategies	Assessment	Standards
Oct. 14	Vocabulary/Word Analysis	*I - 2 Wishes & a truth *A - Human highlighters & KWL chart *M - Role Play activity *C - 3x5 index card for student-generated sentences	Independent practice activity and student-generated sentences using quotation marks & underlining rules	Use knowledge of individual words in unknown compound words to predict their meanings

*I = Inclusion
*A = Attitude
*M = Meaning
*C = Competence

From this outline the team developed detailed lesson plans for the five days using the Motivational Framework for Culturally Responsive Teaching lesson plan template. Exhibit 4.2 (p. 97) shows a sample for one lesson using this format.

EXHIBIT 4.2

Sample Lesson for Benally's Use of the Motivational Framework

The team completed a plan for each lesson. Next, team members implemented the lesson plans with their individual classes. To enhance this process, team members videotaped each other delivering the lesson. This provided an opportunity for the team to reflect on their lessons during grade-level meetings, assess the extent to which each condition of the Motivational Framework (inclusion, attitude, meaning, and competence) were present throughout the lesson, and share instructional expertise for future experimentation.

Team members individually reflected on the following questions during their grade-level meeting:

1. What lesson did you select from your content area and why?

2. How did age, developmental levels, gender, and the culture of your students impact your planning of the lesson?

3. How did you allow for student expression through different performance modes?

4. How did you evaluate the available resources and materials in the lesson?

5. What assessment strategies did you use and why did you select them?

6. What interactions did you have with others (peers, counselors, community agencies) to support your instructions?

7. How has this reflection influenced your instructional practice?

EXHIBIT 4.2 *(continued)*

The Motivational Framework for Culturally Responsive Teaching

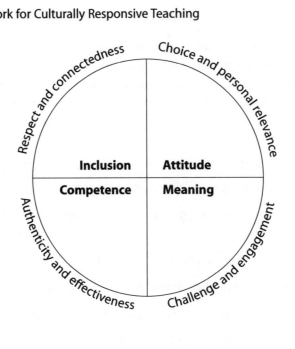

Standards

Vocabulary/word analysis: Use knowledge of individual words in unknown compound words to predict their meanings.

Inclusion

Purpose: To understand compound words and predict their meanings

1. Venn diagram: Draw a Venn diagram on board with a u in the center. Write other words that have a u. Review vowels. Ask for volunteers for words.
2. Card game and practice: Write the words on index cards and write the definition for each word on a separate card. Have students match the words with their definitions.

Attitude

1. Human highlighters: (a) reinforce directions, (b) summarize key points
2. KWL chart: (a) quotation marks and underlining, (b) KWL chart

Meaning

1. Role playing activity
2. Write sentences on the white board. Have students wear hats with quotation marks and have them stand by the board and show where the quotation marks are to be placed.

Competence

1. Independent practice
2. Give each student a 3 x 5 index card and have him or her write a sentence correctly using quotation marks and underlining rules.

Note: Several activities are explained in Creating Highly Motivating Classrooms for All Students:
A Schoolwide Approach to Powerful Teaching with Diverse Learners *(Ginsberg and Wlodkowski, 2000).*
The page numbers can be located in Appendix C.

EXHIBIT 4.3

Process-Folio Organization

Instructions: Read over the following list of chapter contents in a process-folio and decide what you might add or modify.

Chapter One: A list of professional goals and a statement of intention, that is, how you will use the process-folio to contribute to professional goals

Chapter Two: A selected unit plan

Chapter Three: Two or three consecutive motivationally anchored lesson plans from the selected unit with copies of handouts to students

Chapter Four: Samples of student work that represent advanced, proficient, partially proficient, and students with special needs

Chapter Five: Analysis of the unsatisfactory work with ideas for improved learning (Encourage staff to analyze student work with a colleague, using the motivational framework to brainstorm strategies for enhanced learning.)

Chapter Six: A sample approach to record keeping that illustrates how to keep track of student learning (for strategic reteaching)

Chapter Seven: A brief video of a selected lesson

Chapter Eight: A narrative reflection on the video based on personal insights and feedback from a trusted colleague, using the motivational framework

Chapter Nine: Photos of the classroom environment, including bulletin boards and charts

Chapter Ten: Narrative reflection on the portfolio related to professional goals in Chapter One

Chapter Eleven: A roster of literary works and other resources

EXHIBIT 4.4

Walk-Through Agenda

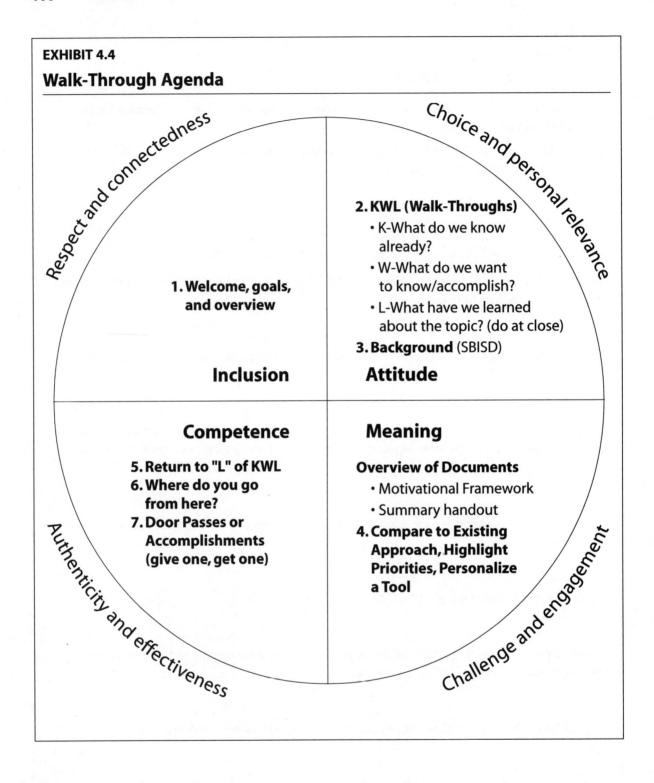

Respect and connectedness

Choice and personal relevance

Inclusion

1. **Welcome, goals, and overview**

Attitude

2. **KWL (Walk-Throughs)**
   - K-What do we know already?
   - W-What do we want to know/accomplish?
   - L-What have we learned about the topic? (do at close)
3. **Background** (SBISD)

Competence

5. **Return to "L" of KWL**
6. **Where do you go from here?**
7. **Door Passes or Accomplishments (give one, get one)**

Meaning

Overview of Documents
   - Motivational Framework
   - Summary handout
4. **Compare to Existing Approach, Highlight Priorities, Personalize a Tool**

Authenticity and effectiveness

Challenge and engagement

EXHIBIT 4.5

Walk-Through Observation Guide

Observer: _____

Teacher: _____

Course and grade level: _____

Date and time:_____

Number of students: _____

1. Is the teacher focusing on standards?   Yes   Somewhat   No
    What did I see?
    (motivational condition: engendering competence)

    _____
    _____
    _____
    _____
    _____

2. What is the level of student engagement?   High (80–100%)   Medium (40–79%)
                                                 Low (0–39%)
    What did I see?
    (motivational condition: enhancing meaning)

    _____
    _____
    _____
    _____
    _____

3. What do the walls of the classroom show? Is the environment pleasant and innovative?
    (motivational conditions: engendering competence, establishing inclusion)

    Do you see displays of the following?

    • Exemplary work

    • Specific scoring criteria (or specific standards and targeted benchmark skills)

    • Writing samples with scoring rubrics

    • Helpful information on mechanics of writing (such as capitalization, punctuation skills)

    • Helpful information on problem solving

    • Classroom agreements (ground rules)

    What did I see?

    _____
    _____
    _____
    _____
    _____

EXHIBIT 4.5 *(continued)*

4. How well do students understand the assignment? (motivational conditions: developing a positive attitude, engendering competence)

    Interviews: Select at least two students to speak with quickly and quietly, either at their desks or in the hallway. Ask them some questions:

    - What are you working on?

    - Why are you working on this?

    - Is what you are working on interesting to you?

    - Is what you are working on in other classes interesting to you?

    - What do you do in this class if you need extra help?

    - Do you have a portfolio? May I see one or two examples of work from this class?

    (Note: Students' answers should go beyond identifying an assignment. The goal is for students to be able to identify the skills they are working on and why. Encourage them to do their best.)

5. Do students communicate effectively and demonstrate critical thinking skills? Do I see evidence of productive communication styles and higher-order questioning? Can students respond in ways that include personal perspectives and imaginative and thoughtful analyses of new information? (motivational conditions: establishing inclusion, enhancing meaning)

    _____

    _____

    _____

    _____

    _____

    _____

Observation Follow-Up

Unless a teacher requests additional time to reflect together on walk-through observations, administrators should keep the walk-through simple. For each of the questions on the walk-through form, the observer might address the following:

- What I noticed

- What questions or compliments I have

- Possibilities that might contribute to equitable and high-quality student learning

Notes:

EXHIBIT 4.6

Walk-Through Summaries

	Student Engagement [a] (circle one)	Wall Walk [b]	Student Interview [c]	Communication and Critical Thinking
Room Number Standards: Evident Not evident	H M L			
Room Number Standards: Evident Not evident	H M L			
Room Number Standards: Evident Not evident	H M L			
Room Number Standards: Evident Not evident	H M L			
Room Number Standards: Evident Not evident	H M L			
Room Number Standards: Evident Not evident	H M L			

[a] *H = high; M = medium; L = low.*

[b] *Look for wall displays of, for example, exemplary work, scoring criteria, writing samples with rubrics, mechanics of writing, problem-solving information, and class agreements.*

[c] *Sample questions include the following: What are you working on? Why are you working on this? Is what you are working on interesting to you? May I see one or two examples of work from this class?*

EXHIBIT 4.7

Overview of Data in a Day

Because all schools struggle with logistical challenges, one of the strengths of the data-in-a-day process is that it lends itself to various adaptations. The following overview is based on approaches that have been most effective for several schools.

Generally, data in a day is a brief self-study that occurs over three days, requiring only one day of substitute coverage for classroom teachers serving on visitation teams. Data in a day begins with an evening dinner to develop a sense of community and prepare teams. Throughout the next day, teams visit classrooms and collect data that they analyze after school with these five questions in mind:

- What are examples of the ways in which teachers are addressing all four conditions of the motivational framework to support students' learning within and across demographic groups?

- With which motivational conditions do teachers demonstrate the most comfort or competence?

- Were any aspects of motivating teaching not apparent during the visits?

- What are some wishes or suggestions that might provide assistance to teachers?

- What insights can students offer in support of or in addition to whatever the team as a whole may have reported?

At the end of the third day, generally just after the school day has ended but before teachers leave for home, data-in-a-day teams share insights with faculty. Insights can be used to stimulate dialogue but also to generate additional forms of inquiry, enhance individual and schoolwide goals, and focus professional development. For example, teams in one school consistently reported the absence of the fourth motivational condition, engendering competence. This stimulated a powerful dialogue about assessment and grading practices and led to an approach in which teachers began sharing and designing more motivationally effective approaches to assessment and grading during the team's planning time. In addition, the school as a whole agreed to grapple with its varying philosophies regarding grading, especially as it relates to research on the limited or negative impact of grades on the performance of low- and middle-performing students (Stiggins, 1988; Wlodkowski and Ginsberg, 1995).

Generally, the process requires eight teams of five people (each consisting of two students, one parent, one teacher, and a team leader) to accurately reflect a school's demographics. Each of these teams visits six different classrooms during the first, second, and third periods for thirty minutes. By the end of the day, teams will have collectively visited forty-eight classrooms. Each team member uses an observation tool that concentrates on one condition of the motivational framework (inclusion, attitude, meaning, or competence). Team members look for ways in which the classroom demonstrates the presence of the condition. At the conclusion of the six classroom visits, team members meet with others who looked for the same motivational condition and share their observations. (For example, all of the people who looked for establishing inclusion meet to compare notes.)

After they compare results, look for trends, and identify both areas of strength and areas that seem to need support in order to increase student success, they develop a way to share information with the whole faculty. They share this information at the end of the school day that follows the classroom visitation day.

EXHIBIT 4.8

Action-Research Approach Based on School Renewal Questions

Step One: Select a Focus

This example is based on the approach an instructional leadership cadre used to practice action research and simultaneously further schoolwide goals. Each member of the cadre chose one of the following questions to explore:

- To what extent does our school have a shared purpose or vision?

  (Sample hypothesis: A shared understanding of what a highly motivating school looks like can help us pull in the same direction to come closer to our goals of student success.)

- To what extent is classroom learning highly motivating and relevant to all students?

- To what extent do we systematically engage in collaborative adult learning?

- To what extent does our school encourage diverse parents and community members to participate in meaningful ways?

- To what extent do we have an effective way to negotiate conflict among ourselves?

Your question and hypothesis:

_____
_____
_____
_____
_____
_____
_____
_____
_____
_____
_____
_____

Step Two: Collect Data

The team members helped each other develop ways to collect data. For each question, team members used three different kinds of data, including the following:

- Surveys
- Oral interviews
- Classroom observations
- Examinations of student work

EXHIBIT 4.8 *(continued)*

This part of the process included a time line outlining when and how the team would collect data.

Your approach: _____

_____

_____

_____

_____

_____

_____

_____

_____

Step Three: Analyze and Interpret the Data

Team members helped each other analyze and interpret data and decided to create posters to display in the faculty lounge as a way to share results with fellow colleagues.

Findings and Ways to Exhibit Findings: _____

_____

_____

_____

_____

_____

_____

_____

_____

Step Four: Take Action

After sharing findings with colleagues, the team worked with the school to refine its approach to ongoing renewal. Team members published their action-research plans, findings, and new hypotheses in a booklet for parents and community members.

Next Steps: Ideas for New Questions and Approaches _____

_____

_____

_____

_____

_____

_____

_____

_____

EXHIBIT 4.9

Sample Action-Research Approach Related to Classroom Practice

Question One: How do my student-assessment practices affect student learning and performance? (motivational condition: engendering competence)

Hypothesis: If I facilitate the use of ongoing, authentic feedback regarding student learning for students, parents, and myself, then students will be more likely to produce higher quality work more often.

Methods: I will do the following:

- Review the chapter on engendering competence in *Diversity and Motivation* (Wlodkowski and Ginsberg, 1995)

- Design and share form and content of assessment before instruction

- Use multiple formal and informal assessment methods to support and assess student strengths, needs, and performance and to influence instructional design

- Provide students with multiple opportunities to demonstrate high-quality work by using a "scaffolding" approach to instruction and student skill and knowledge development

- Increase guided practice and collaborative group-learning opportunities

- Include independent performance opportunities within each scaffolded learning experience

Evidence: I will gather evidence by tracking and comparing some or all of the following indicators each quarter over the course of the year:

- Percentage of student work turned in per assignment

- IAS common skill assessment data

- Six traits, reading, primary and secondary sources, oral presentation, PowerPoint, seminar

- Colorado Workplace Competency assessment (CWE) data

- Grades (IAS and CWE)

- Lesson plans developed

- Rubrics designed

- Student reflections

Question Two: How do grading practices affect student motivation and productivity? (motivational condition: engendering competence)

Hypothesis: If students have opportunities to practice skills and knowledge in a setting that provides feedback without grades, they will be more likely to turn in work, take risks, and improve performance on graded assessments.

EXHIBIT 4.9 *(continued)*

Methods: I will read the section on feedback in *Creating Highly Motivating Classrooms for All Students* (Ginsberg and Wlodkowski, 2000) and develop my own feedback policy to enhance the clarity and consistency of feedback I provide to students. I will develop a brief survey to elicit student feedback on my feedback. Also, students will receive credit for the ways in which they self-assess class assignments and major projects. This will count as participation and will account for 30 percent of each student's grade. The assessment for major projects will be broken down to provide a lot of feedback to students and allow them to practice emerging skills prior to the final assessments. I hope this will help them feel safer and more successful, thus improving assessment scores.

Evidence: I will gather evidence by comparing this year's grade book to last year's, in the areas of percentages of assignments turned in as well as assessment scores. I will also gather anecdotal evidence through student interviews and personal observations about student motivation.

Note: These are adapted from the work of Jan Herrera, Stafford Boyd and David Weisbart at Thornton High School, Thornton, Colorado.

Suggestions and comments:

EXHIBIT 4.10

Matrix for Rubiner's Use of Data to Implement School Renewal

School Goal	Measures	Data to Collect	Collector(s) of Data
Goal one: 80% of students who have attended for three or more years will meet or exceed state standards.	• SAT-9 • SABE • District writing assessments • Weekly grade-level assessments, unit assessments	• SAT-9, SABE, district writing assessment, grade-level weekly assessments, unit assessments • Reading and math scores • Number of years in program • Language proficiency • Free or reduced lunch • Gender and ethnicity • Attendance, retention, and detention • Extracurricular activities • Level of parent involvement	• Teachers • Principal • District coordinator
Goal two: 75% of students who've attended for less than three years will meet or exceed state standards.	• Comparison of students in grades 1-3 • Comparison of students in grades 4-6	• Student identification • Number of years in literacy program • Teacher and grade levels • Language proficiency • Free or reduced lunch • Gender and ethnicity • Attendance, retention, and detention • Extracurricular activities • Level of parent involvement	• Teachers • Principal • District coordinator
Goal three: 80% of staff will show knowledge of instructional strategies and apply the motivational framework.	• Lesson plans • Monthly family nights (records) • Staff meetings (records) • Professional development (documents) • Grade-level meetings (summaries and samples of student work) • Student evaluations • Videotaped lessons • Classroom observations	• Videotapes scored by school-based panel • Schoolwide review of lesson plans • Parent feedback • Teacher surveys • Agendas and minutes • Student surveys	• Teachers • Principal • District coordinator

EXHIBIT 4.10 *(continued)*

School Goal	Measures	Data to Collect	Collector(s) of Data
Goal four: Rubiner families will develop a sense of connectedness and collaborate in the children's education.	• Parent volunteers • Two-way parent communication • Parent surveys • Parent-teacher conferences • Open house (records)	• Parent-class involvement logs • Parent surveys and interviews • Parent focus groups • Attendance logs • Parent-teacher contact records • Lesson plans for literacy nights and other learning opportunities based on the motivational framework • Parent demographics	• Teachers • Principal • District coordinator
Goal five: 60% of students who attended for less than one year will meet or exceed state standards.	• SAT-9 and state assessment • ELLs • State ELL assessment • District writing assessments • Grade level weekly, unit, and theme assessments	• State assessments • District writing assessment • Grade-level weekly, unit, and theme assessments • Reading and math scores • Gender and ethnicity • Number of years in program • Language proficiency • Free or reduced lunch • Attendance, retention, and detention • Extracurricular activities • Level of parent involvement • ELL status	• Teachers • Principal • District coordinator

Notes:

EXHIBIT 4.11

Rubric for Assessing Lesson Design Using the Motivational Framework

! = exceeds standards   √ = adequate   ? = approaching

	!	√	?
Clarity of Lesson	Selects most appropriate location for strategies.	Needs some clarification.	Unclear.
Quality of Strategies	Strategies for addressing identified standards "hit on all fours" in meaningful and imaginative ways.	Strategies are appropriate for addressing identified standards.	Unclear, more information would help.
Opportunities for Differentiation	Indicates opportunities for all students to develop interests and skills.	Indicates opportunities for most students to develop interests and skills.	May limit challenge and success by focusing primarily on one student group.
Equitable Assessment	Clear and fair criteria for success with opportunities for self-assessment.	Criteria for success is a bit vague but there are opportunities for self-assessment.	Criteria for success is not evident, nor are opportunities for self-assessment.

EXHIBIT 4.12

Annual Time Line for School Renewal

Months	Task(s)	Participants
August and September	Convene school-based evaluation team. Agree on work plan for the year. Communicate with staff regarding team purpose regularly. Finalize evaluation benchmarks and gain staff commitment to these benchmarks. Establish a method for tracking parent-teacher contacts, parent attendance at school events, parent involvement with child's education. Prepare staff agreement on plan to complete ongoing in-depth analyses on state assessment results. Begin documenting staff development opportunities in which staff members have participated. Finalize motivational framework scoring rubric for teacher videotapes. Clarify student tenure measure and student mobility by creating a method for tracking attendance and mobility.	School-based evaluation team District coordinator
October	Document the leadership team's efforts to facilitate the teaching staff's use of the motivational framework. Develop a method for observing and tracking the classroom use of effective instruction and motivational framework. Collect data on all parent activities, parent-teacher contacts, and parents' involvement in their child's education. Conduct more in-depth data analyses on state assessments administered to students.	School-based evaluation team School principal District coordinator
November and December	Collect data. Prepare for spring interviews of teachers and parents. Revise survey instruments for teachers, parents, and students.	School-based evaluation team School principal District coordinator
January and February	Report on current findings from data collected. Collect data on teacher fidelity to implementation of motivational framework and effective instruction.	School-based evaluation team School principal District coordinator
March	Conduct parent and teacher surveys.	School-based evaluation team School principal District coordinator

EXHIBIT 4.12 *(continued)*

Months	Task(s)	Participants
April	Conduct parent and teacher interviews. Complete student surveys in identified grade levels. Collect data on teacher fidelity to implementation of motivational framework and effective instruction.	School-based evaluation team School principal District coordinator
May and June	Tally information on parent-teacher contacts. Present findings from surveys and interviews. Communicate in-progress results to teaching staff and parents.	School-based evaluation team School principal District coordinator
June and July	Analyze data. Draft evaluation report. Circulate draft report to principal and staff members for review and corrections. Write report to state on Comprehensive School Reform Demonstration status.	School-based evaluation team School principal District coordinator
August	Submit final evaluation report.	School-based evaluation team School principal District coordinator

A special thank you is extended to Pablo Fiene at Alum Rock Union Elementary School District in San Jose, California, for this exhibit.

Notes:

EXHIBIT 4.13

Teacher Survey: Being a Highly Motivating School

Instructions: Identify the degree to which you agree or disagree with each statement (1 = strongly disagree; 5 = strongly agree).

Statement	1	2	3	4	5
Students are encouraged to participate in class regularly.	1	2	3	4	5
Class time is used for the students to work collaboratively.	1	2	3	4	5
I speak personally to each student about his or her academic progress.	1	2	3	4	5
Students who consistently cause problems should not be in class.	1	2	3	4	5
Students are encouraged to set personal goals for their learning.	1	2	3	4	5
Using teachable moments is an important part of instruction.	1	2	3	4	5
Students have a choice in how their learning will be assessed.	1	2	3	4	5
Students may select whom they work with in class.	1	2	3	4	5
Students are expected to do high-quality work.	1	2	3	4	5
Tapping into a student's prior knowledge is not important when beginning a new lesson or unit.	1	2	3	4	5
Engaged students are a sign of a successful lesson.	1	2	3	4	5
Expectations for excellent final products are made clear to all students.	1	2	3	4	5
Students are provided opportunities to assess their own growth as learners.	1	2	3	4	5
A deliberate effort is made to connect classroom learning to the real world.	1	2	3	4	5
School calendar activities (such as assemblies, plays, holidays, and celebrations) reflect the ethnic and cultural diversity of this city's community.	1	2	3	4	5
Our curriculum incorporates values, attitudes, and behavior that support ethnic and cultural pluralism (such as equality and social justice).	1	2	3	4	5
Teachers and administrators have high-quality professional development opportunities aligned with clear and purposeful educational and multicultural goals.	1	2	3	4	5
Parents and community members from various ethnic and cultural backgrounds are encouraged to participate in classroom and schoolwide activities in meaningful ways.	1	2	3	4	5
Our school has a systematic process for checking our progress toward meeting schoolwide goals.	1	2	3	4	5
Our school has a cohesive overall plan to achieve the school's education goals, to narrow the achievement gap among our student groups, and to strengthen learning for all students.	1	2	3	4	5
Schoolwide teaching and learning strategies have been deliberated and established for all students.	1	2	3	4	5
We have a schoolwide vision about the role of ethnic and cultural diversity within our school.	1	2	3	4	5
Our staff is well informed of its progress on continuous school improvement.	1	2	3	4	5
Our staff has been involved in continuous school improvement.	1	2	3	4	5

EXHIBIT 4.14

Teacher Survey: Taking Personal Responsibility

Instructions: Identify the degree to which you agree or disagree with each statement (1 = strongly disagree; 5 = strongly agree).

Awareness	I am aware of how the motivational framework applies to our school improvement goals.	1	2	3	4	5
	I can articulate the motivational framework.	1	2	3	4	5
	I can name specific instructional strategies that relate to each of the four conditions.	1	2	3	4	5
Depth of Understanding & Personal Application	I apply the motivational framework to lesson design.	1	2	3	4	5
	I apply the motivational framework to daily instruction.	1	2	3	4	5
	I use the motivational framework to be more reflective about my teaching.	1	2	3	4	5
	I use the motivational framework to help my teaching become increasingly equitable and responsive.	1	2	3	4	5
Transfer to Others	I can teach the motivational framework to someone else.	1	2	3	4	5
	When I work with my grade-level team to plan lessons or solve problems, I refer to the motivational framework.	1	2	3	4	5
	When we as a team design schoolwide learning opportunities, we try to explicitly address issues related to equity.	1	2	3	4	5
	When we as a team work with the school on planning, we incorporate the motivational framework.	1	2	3	4	5
	We have made a schoolwide commitment to using the motivational framework in lesson design.	1	2	3	4	5
	We have made a schoolwide commitment to using the motivational framework to reflect on our teaching.	1	2	3	4	5

EXHIBIT 4.15

Monthly Report: Professional Development Activities to Enhance Teaching Strategies

Staff Development Strategies	What Was Provided? By Whom?	Date of Receipt	Number of Hours Spent
Professional development activities to support school goals			
Professional development activities to support implementation of the motivational framework			
Professional development activities to support implementation of curriculum content and performance standards			
Professional development activities related to student assessment and performance monitoring			
Teachers as trainers, mentors, or coaches			
Informal classroom observations among teachers			
Informal classroom observations by leadership team members			
School Support Teams			
Special teaching strategies for special populations			
Increased cultural awareness			

EXHIBIT 4.15 *(continued)*

Increased preparation to use educational technology for instruction			
Professional development activities related to instructional strategies			
Strategies for teaching to content standards			
Instructional strategies for teaching: • Low-achieving students • English learners • Migrant students • Native American students			
Strategies to increase parent involvement in student learning			
Strategies for encouraging self-discipline and respect			
Leadership development			
Adapting teaching to meet reading and math requirements			
Use of technology			
Shadowing of master teachers			
Instruction related to curriculum and subject-area content			

EXHIBIT 4.16

Student Survey

Instructions: Rate your agreement or disagreement with the statements below by circling a number from 1 to 5 (1 = strongly disagree; 5 = strongly agree).

Relevance to real world					
I feel that I am learning valuable information in class.	1	2	3	4	5
My teachers are providing real-life things for me to learn about.	1	2	3	4	5
What I learn in my classes is useful in the real world.	1	2	3	4	5
How the teachers treat me					
My teachers pay as much attention to me as they do to other students.	1	2	3	4	5
I feel all students are treated fairly and rules are applied equally to all students.	1	2	3	4	5
I feel that I am a valued part of the class.	1	2	3	4	5
I feel respected by my teachers and classmates.	1	2	3	4	5
My teachers are interested in my ideas.	1	2	3	4	5
My teachers expect me to do well.	1	2	3	4	5
Classroom learning environment					
I can choose my preferred way of learning something.	1	2	3	4	5
The class is interesting to me.	1	2	3	4	5
I feel comfortable and confident showing others what I have learned.	1	2	3	4	5
Feeling successful in my classes helps me learn.	1	2	3	4	5

Anything else you'd like your teachers to know?

EXHIBIT 4.17

Sample Student Survey Results

	Strongly Disagree				Strongly Agree
Relevance to real world	1	2	3	4	5
I feel that I am learning valuable information in class.					
Third Grade	2%	2%	15%	32%	49%
Fourth Grade	1%	5%	12%	26%	56%
Fifth Grade	2%	2%	16%	47%	33%
Sixth Grade	3%	6%	26%	36%	28%
Total of all grades	2%	4%	16%	34%	43%

Observations and insights:

EXHIBIT 4.18

Parent Survey

Instructions: Rate your agreement or disagreement with the statements below by circling a number from 1 to 5 (1 = strongly disagree; 5 = strongly agree) or circling "Don't know."

Inclusion						
Information is communicated frequently and well.	1	2	3	4	5	Don't know
My child is treated fairly at school.	1	2	3	4	5	Don't know
I feel my child is safe in school.	1	2	3	4	5	Don't know
I feel that my child and I are welcome in school.	1	2	3	4	5	Don't know
The school is responsive to students' needs and interests.	1	2	3	4	5	Don't know
Leadership in this school is visible and strong.	1	2	3	4	5	Don't know
Parents are involved in making decisions in this school.	1	2	3	4	5	Don't know
Attitude						
The principal is interested in my concerns and problems.	1	2	3	4	5	Don't know
School staff members are available for conferences, and I have opportunities to voice my concerns.	1	2	3	4	5	Don't know
Teachers in this school seem to like being here.	1	2	3	4	5	Don't know
My child shows a feeling of excitement about going to school.	1	2	3	4	5	Don't know
I am satisfied with the level of homework required of my child.	1	2	3	4	5	Don't know
People I know speak favorably about this school.	1	2	3	4	5	Don't know
Meaning						
I am given opportunities to be involved in my child's education in ways that I enjoy.	1	2	3	4	5	Don't know
My child seems bored at school.	1	2	3	4	5	Don't know
This school has high expectations for all students.	1	2	3	4	5	Don't know
I am enriched by my experiences with the school.	1	2	3	4	5	Don't know
Competence						
Teacher expectations are clear and understandable to my child.	1	2	3	4	5	Don't know
I am frequently informed about my child's progress.	1	2	3	4	5	Don't know
I am happy with my child's progress in school.	1	2	3	4	5	Don't know
This school places a high value on student success and achievement.	1	2	3	4	5	Don't know
My child feels successful at this school.	1	2	3	4	5	Don't know
I believe my participation at this school makes a big difference.	1	2	3	4	5	Don't know
This school helps me do a better job supporting my child's education.	1	2	3	4	5	Don't know

EXHIBIT 4.19

Parent-Teacher Contact Log

Teacher's Name and Room Number: _____

Month: _____

Date	Parent Name	Purpose	P	F	L	SF	O

P: Telephone contact　　　　**F:** Face to face contact

L: Letter or written contact　　**SF:** Student folder notes with work that is sent home

O: Other form of contact

EXHIBIT 4.20

Parent Involvement Log

Teacher's Name and Room Number: _____

Month: _____

Parent Involvement Strategies	What Was Provided and to Whom?	Date	Time Involved in Implementing Strategy
Work with parents to set learning goals for their children.			
Initiate face-to-face meetings with parents.			
Initiate phone calls to parents when a child is having problems or not having problems.			
Recommend services to parents such as parent resource centers or family training.			
Show parents models of successful student work.			
Discuss individual student assessment results with parents.			
Ask parents to review and sign homework.			
Provide weekly activities so that students work with parents to reinforce what was taught in class.			

EXHIBIT 4.20 *(continued)*

Invite parents to present to the class about their experiences and beliefs and to share skills and talent with students.			
All parents sign parent-school compact.			
Help parents understand where their child should be academically and what he or she should be able to do at this grade level.			
Explain to parents education standards and expectations for grade performance.			
Make home visits.			

Follow-up notes:

EXHIBIT 4.21

Standard and Criterion Score: Measurement and Geometry

Standard	MG 1.0 [a]	MG 1.0 [b]	MG 2.0 [c]	MG 2.1 [d]
Criterion Score	6/9	3/4	2/3	3/5
Student Name				

[a] Standard 1.0: Students understand that measurement is accomplished by identifying a unit of measure, iterating or repeating that unit and comparing it to the item to be measured.

[b] Standard 1.3: Students measure the length of an object to the nearest inch and centimeter.

[c] Standard 2.0: Students identify and describe the attributes of common figures in the plane and of common objects in space.

[d] Standard 2.1: Students describe and classify plane and solid geometric shapes according to the number of faces, edges, and vertices.

EXHIBIT 4.22

Standards and Test Preparation: Getting Creative

Joseph Butler's grade-level team recently decided it needed to strengthen its clarity about and use of the state's language arts standards. Team members discussed this at their weekly grade-level meeting. Before beginning, they reviewed their schoolwide communication agreement, which emphasizes the norm of maintaining a hopeful, problem-solving orientation. They wanted to avoid complaining about the emphasis that is widely placed on the state test.

The team wanted to find a way not only to help students learn about and apply standards but to do so in a way that supported their motivation. Using the motivational framework as a guide, team members decided to review language arts standards with their students, using the district's new standards-focused report card as a guide. Each fourth-grade teacher then asked a pair of students (establishing inclusion) to write a different standard on a sentence strip. Next, each teacher asked students to create two sentence strips for each language arts standard: one defining the standard and one giving an original example or application of the standard (developing a positive attitude and enhancing meaning). Students color-coded the two sentence strips: yellow for the standard's definition and green for the example or application. This process, the teachers believed, would help to heighten student and teacher awareness of and use of standards.

But they also wanted to find a way to help students to prove to themselves that they could demonstrate learning in a multiple-choice format. They had been noticing that students quickly tuned out on standardized tests when they got bored or frustrated with the content or format. As one way to create positive practice with and associations related to a common testing format, they developed an activity they called post office. This is a weekly round-robin between fourth-grade classes in which each class develops for another class three multiple-choice questions based on a standard that the monthly language arts unit assessment has identified as one in which the class needs reinforcement. Friday mornings, each class posts the questions it has developed on the door of a designated classroom. Friday afternoons, students in the other class return their responses to the class that authored the questions, and that class determines whether the answers are correct. They chart the number of correct responses.

The post-office activity, this team hoped, would contribute to establishing community schoolwide, helping classrooms to connect to each other. In addition, the activity can heighten students' attitudes toward standardized test formats because this approach to test preparation offers choice through test construction and personal relevance through peer pressure and support. Further, it contributes to the motivational conditions of enhancing meaning and engendering competence, because students apply what they have learned to a common format that makes success concrete.

Note: A special thank you to the 2002–2003 fourth-grade team at Cureton Elementary School in Alum Rock, California, for inspiring this case study.

EXHIBIT 4.23

Draft Statement of Purpose for the School Process-Folio

We are building the school portfolio in order to establish one document that describes the overall school plan; documents growth being made in student learning and schoolwide (organizational) effectiveness; guides the school's unique approach to continuous improvement; provides examples of standards-based, motivationally anchored teaching and learning; builds collegial reflection and confidence; and helps communicate with local, regional, and state constituencies.

Notes:

EXHIBIT 4.24

Draft Structure of the School Process-Folio

Chapter One: Description of the school, including photographs, creative documents, and artifacts that bring the school to life

Chapter Two: The school's renewal plan

Chapter Three: The leadership team: statement of purpose, minutes, meeting agendas, schoolwide communication agreement, and other accomplishments

Chapter Four: Faculty roster and expertise

Chapter Five: Sample standards-based lessons using the motivational framework

Chapter Six: Data (conventional data such as standardized test scores and creative data such as data-in-a-day)

Chapter Seven: Schoolwide collaboration and professional development

Chapter Eight: Parent, community, and district involvement

Chapter Nine: Signature development and results: what the school can be known for nationally, a unique identity that is the school's rallying point (Examples include service learning, literacy across the curriculum, or integrating the arts.)

Notes:

EXHIBIT 4.25

The Poster Conference

What is a poster conference?

A *poster conference* is an efficient and interactive method for sharing displays, ideas, and questions related to a central topic or theme. Participants create posters that represent the design and evolution of their initiatives, sample courses or lessons based on the motivational framework, culturally responsive teaching strategies, and other applications of learning. Initiative participants and guests engage in dialogue about display topics, elaborating about aspects of what they are learning and most value.

Who might attend?

People who might attend include, but are not limited to, poster-conference presenters, other educators, district personnel, students, parents and family members, and other community members.

How might people interact?

The process can be informal, with half the presenters and other participants selecting displays to visit and spontaneously engaging in dialogue with display presenters. (After a given time, the remaining presenters visit displays and engage in dialogue with attendees.) Presenters should provide a one-page summary of their display topic for guests who visit their display. Dialogue or feedback sheets are distributed in a welcome packet. These provide presenters with explicit feedback from display visitors. On the feedback sheet, for example, visitors might be asked to submit a written response to display presenters on such topics as (1) something learned from this display that is of particular value, (2) a recommendation for enhanced effectiveness with topics presented, (3) suggestions for how the display might influence participation or personal practice of a student, parent, educator, or community member.

Customize a draft statement of purpose for your poster conference:

Chapter 5

Developing a Signature with Advocacy to Support It

AMID MOBILITY, FATIGUE, and competing commitments, school renewal occasionally plateaus. One of the ways to maintain focus is through signature and advocacy. *Signature* is a theme that excites a school community and integrates academic goals. Schools ask themselves: What do we want to model for the nation as a visionary demonstration site? Examples include community learning, literacy across the curriculum, technology and publishing, or as illustrated in Exhibit 5.2, integrating arts and literacy.

This stimulates ongoing renewal, but it also helps public schools transcend their emerging reputation as the place that students attend if their families cannot afford alternatives. In a time of negative publicity, charter schools, and privatization, for a school to be seen as a distinct and exciting leader in the field of education is essential if public education is to survive.

Advocacy refers to the support that schools need at all levels of the school community: students, families, community members, and district personnel. Innovation requires advocacy. Examples of ways to develop advocacy are data in a day (Chapter Four, Activity Three), lesson studies (Chapter Three, Activity Three), support for school-based literacy and reform coaches (Chapter Two, Activities Five through Eight), and attendance at the annual poster conference (Chapter Four, Activity Nine). Assuring that parents and district representatives also serve on the instructional leadership team is key. Parents are able to rally the community, and district representatives are essential for garnering district-level support for innovation. The personal ways they communicate are essential to the development and sustainability of new ideas.

The following activities help schools initially think through notions about signature and advocacy. Both of the case studies illustrate that the notion of signature must be integrated into school goals. Add-on programs tend to have marginal, if any, influence on schoolwide curriculum and instruction.

Activity One: Generating Ideas and Advocacy for Signature

Purpose   To encourage staff to think outside the box to elaborate on and support their vision of teaching and learning

Participants   Instructional staff in teams of five or six

Time   Forty-five minutes

Materials   Handouts of Exhibit 5.1 (p. 133) and Exhibit 5.2 or 5.3 (pp. 134–137), newsprint, markers, and masking tape for carousel graffiti

Process

a theme that excites school community
some of Vision
no

Sure

Step one: Define the notion of signature. Ask participants to work in pairs to share their understanding using the graphic in Figure 5.1.

Step two: As a large group, read the case study of Zinn Middle School (Exhibit 5.2) or King High School (Exhibit 5.3). Please note that both can be adapted to elementary, middle, or high school. Also note that the King case study provides a more in-depth overview of school goals. King is based on a composite of outstanding schools and represents an ideal that would be challenging, if desirable, to create. This is important to mention to participants because many educators are understandably sensitive about how people compare schools to one another. The purpose of the case study is to stimulate ideas that can help a school community build on its own accomplishments.

Step three: Ask people to pair with a different partner to talk about what they found to be interesting, how they believe the Zinn signature of literacy and the arts or the King signature of service learning contributes to overarching schoolwide goals. Ask participants to consider how a signature might contribute to goals at their own school.

Step four: Ask each group to brainstorm its initial question using carousel graffiti (see Chapter Two), and at your signal, pass their paper to the next group on the right. Before beginning, review each question to ensure that teams similarly interpret their meaning. Questions include the following:

- What talents are accessible to us in our parent and teacher community?

- What are some potential signature options for our school?

- How could we use the notion of signature to enhance student learning?

- How could we use the notion of signature to strengthen professional collaboration?

- How might we find time to enhance collaboration?

Step five: Transcribe the graffiti responses. At the next staff meeting, distribute the transcriptions and ask participants to focus on the page that lists potential signature options. Ask them to put a star by their first choice, a check by their second choice, and an X by the choice they do not like at all.

Step six: Ask staff to transfer their codes to a large transcription of options posted on the wall.

Step seven: Ask staff to note trends. Narrow the choices according to the trends. Work with staff to reach consensus on a signature decision.

Step eight: Work with the instructional leadership cadre to draft a plan based on staff interests.

Districts as Advocates for Innovation

Along with the role of the principal, the role of the district is attracting attention for educational innovation. The achievements of the schools in both the case studies, for example, could not occur without district-level advocacy. District staff makes an enormous difference in whether a school sees change as an opportunity or an act of compliance. When schools attempt innovation as an act of compliance, they are likely to take the most cursory approach to accomplishing their goals. The threat of extrinsic sanctions operates in much the same way with school improvement as it does in classroom learning. Such sanctions may work in the short term, but the by-products generally include resentment, sabotage, or amnesia.

At the same time, schools need goals, benchmarks, strategies, and assessments to engage in substantive restructuring. This is especially true in districts experiencing large turnover in faculty and administrators. Schools cannot move forward if they are forever starting over. Add to that the requirements of special funding, such as comprehensive school reform monies. Established criteria or expectations are essential for continued revenue as well as for success.

School districts often walk a delicate line between assuring the district is meeting the contractual requirements of special programs and serving as a support for a school's spirit of invention. Of course, meeting state requirements and encouraging creativity are not mutually exclusive. But it is easy to slip from a primary role of being creative to one of merely monitoring, when so many programs require attention and so many reports need updating. Successful school renewal is imaginative as well as research-based, and it requires focus at all levels. The district best serves schools when the liaison attends school-based sessions of leadership-team work and is willing to learn, model, coach, and reflect alongside school-based change advocates.

There are many impressive examples of district leadership. One such example is a federal program coordinator who serves as a coach to school-based reform coaches. Although this was something he had never tried, he set aside competing demands and worked with the school coaches to customize the process-folio process described in Chapter Four. The team developed lesson plans based on the motivational framework. And as a trusted colleague, he observed demonstration lessons and cofacilitated lesson studies until the school-based coaches developed confidence in their new roles. The courage to seek something better requires the courage to learn in partnership.

Summary

The emphasis of this book has been on strategies for educators to use to implement motivationally anchored renewal that supports student learning. To that end this book has presented renewal strategies embedded in an intrinsic theory of motivation, one that is understood to serve people within and across cultural groups in educational environments. Public education may not be able to redress injustices for which all of society should bear responsibility, but rethinking instruction from a motivational perspective can ignite imagination and hope. In the words of a respected colleague, the absence of hope is morally corrupt. The many powerful examples of school communities that mobilize their strength through unity and creativity will serve as an inspiration for all of us.

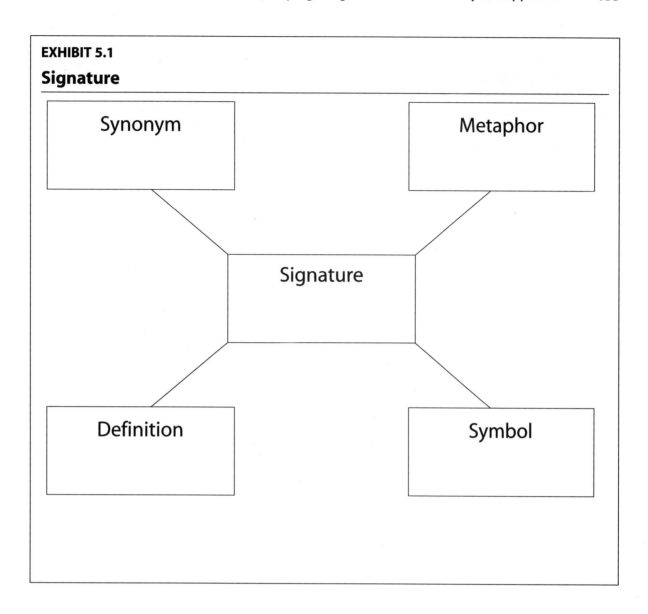

EXHIBIT 5.1

Signature

EXHIBIT 5.2

Zinn Middle School

Zinn Middle School serves its community as a comprehensive arts and literacy demonstration site. Grounded in research on intrinsic motivation, culturally responsive teaching, and standards-based instruction, Zinn approaches ongoing renewal with the creativity and inventiveness of the entire school community. With quantitative and qualitative data as evidence of students' success, Zinn anchors its commitment to self-expression and creativity among students and staff in its district's literacy and math standards.

Visitors to Zinn observe students, parents, community members, and staff eagerly engaged in learning that elicits will as well as skill. Teachers have agreed to eight "givens" to support learning: respectful interactions, peer collaboration, clear purpose, personal goals, cultural relevance, creative projects focused on solving challenging real-world problems, assessment criteria that all Zinn students understand, and self-assessment. These goals are also embedded in everyday teaching, in the arts and literacy block, and in the creation of an original bilingual opera.

As with the arts and literacy block, Zinn Production Company, the student-run opera company, unites children across grade levels and programs such as bilingual immersion, monolingual English, and special education. This approach has the additional benefit of enhancing the pervasive family atmosphere. Discipline referrals have sharply dropped, and attendance has steadily improved.

Classroom teachers support student motivation through a comprehensive and ongoing approach to professional development that is a part of daily practice. With a shared instructional language informed by the motivational framework for culturally responsive teaching, teachers collaboratively plan, implement, and reflect on instruction. This occurs during daily planning time; every Wednesday afternoon, when students are released early from school; and in visits to each other's classrooms for demonstrations and collegial support. Teachers further carry out this approach by planning and team-teaching weekly arts and literacy classes and six-week lesson sets, each of which concludes with a day in which students present demonstrations of learning to the community.

To understand their success and challenges, teachers analyze data from conventional sources such as standardized test scores and teacher-written assessments. But as part of a network of schools committed to inter- and intraschool innovation and communication, Zinn teachers also examine student work and design action-research projects. Known as the cycle of inquiry, this process allows teachers to examine and apply the influence of schoolwide creativity on daily practice. For example, teachers might work together to distill the characteristics that make the arts and literacy block classes of, for example, dramatic reading, tai chi, or teaching of the Filipino cultural dance known as *tinikling* of high interest to a range of students. They then apply these principles to daily language arts and math, collect data about improved student achievement, and learn from their findings.

An instructional leadership cadre comprising teachers and parents from a range of programs coordinates teacher learning. The cadre serves as the professional development arm of the school-improvement team. All teachers have input into the design of professional development through team representatives. As well, the entire faculty, with parent representation, reviews and approves the school-improvement plan, with professional development as a central component. The school-improvement plan is a cohesive, working document that helps Zinn Middle School maintain its vision and focus on motivation, standards-based learning, and the arts.

Adapted from the work of Grimmer Elementary School in Fremont, California.

EXHIBIT 5.3

King High School

King High School is located in a rural agricultural community fifty miles from a large city. Its students are from diverse backgrounds. Approximately 50 percent speak English as a second language, and 45 percent are members of migrant families. Approximately 85 percent of the student population qualifies for free or reduced lunch.

examples?

For some time King High School educators, parents, and community members have been working together as an adult learning community to study, develop, and apply highly motivating, culturally responsive pedagogy to support the academic accomplishment of all students. It has eliminated pull-out programs that require teachers to label students and limit their regular classroom instruction. Teachers have agreed to share responsibility for all students through pedagogy that allows students to be motivated learners and valued community members. In fact, motivation to learn and serve is the signature of the King High School community.

To contribute to this, the school maintains a large literacy center that is staffed on a rotating basis by faculty, parents, and members of local organizations. The center is a haven in many ways. Students and families who are in the process of acquiring English visit the center, which remains open in the evening, to develop reading, writing, and oral language skills. However, students of all kinds frequently stop by for one-on-one assistance with assignments or to work together in the tea-house area. In the tea house, which students have designed and maintain, hot water for tea and hot chocolate is always available. It is not uncommon to see students meeting there with their advocate. An *advocate* is an adult friend who knows a few students well and provides personal support for success throughout a student's stay at King. Students also drop by the literacy center to join in ongoing book discussions, plan community-based projects with local artists and other service-learning volunteers, observe demonstrations, contribute to technology-based projects that are routinely facilitated by visiting scientists, engage in independent research, or read silently on the comfortable pillows in the fiction loft. The center is particularly proud of its ability to stimulate student interest and consciousness by offering a broad range of literature by ethnically and culturally diverse authors.

a lot of parent involvement

Not only does the literacy center respond to student and community interests, it also provides a context for teachers to learn new ways to support literacy across the curriculum. At least once a month, each teacher can be released from regular duty to serve as a volunteer coach in the literacy center. This helps to fine-tune faculty's ability to teach literacy skills and encourages strong, consistent expectations for high-quality reading and writing across the curriculum. In fact, King High School has created a literacy rubric that guides skill development in the center and defines expectations for high-quality writing in all courses.

Adult members of the school community are especially committed to learning that builds confidence and motivation through teamwork, creativity, problem solving, and community action. Its vision statement, displayed on a banner over the front door, reads: "King High School is a highly motivating, caring learning environment where youth and adults work together to strengthen their skills, maximize their potential, and contribute to the community."

The school has developed a model for supporting adult learning toward this vision. Teacher teams regularly learn together. Recently, each teacher has agreed to become closely acquainted with two historically low-performing students from backgrounds other than his or her own. Teachers will eat lunch with these students once a week, meet individually with them regularly, conduct home visits, and stay in touch with parents to learn more about each student's strengths and challenges. Teachers will use their awareness to create lesson plans designed to support the motivation of their two students. In addition, they will identify a team member to observe the students as the lessons are being implemented and to observe the highest-achieving students as well. At team meetings they will discuss observations and collaborate to strengthen instructional practice by examining student work. These adult-learning teams listen to whomever is presenting a piece of work to understand student characteristics as well as influences on the student—such as the environment, instructions, and support—that may have contributed to the final product. Together, they brainstorm ideas that could strengthen student motivation, knowledge, and skill. The emphasis is on strengthening the motivational conditions that influence success rather than on "fixing" the student. Using the motivational framework for culturally responsive teaching, they consider the following questions:

- What might be done to create a stronger sense of respect and connectedness—or emotional safety—among all students?
- How might the choices offered and the personal relevance of the content be strengthened?
- How might the learning experience more effectively challenge and engage this student to the extent that the student might actually lose track of time?
- How might the assessment process create authentic evidence of emerging skills to encourage a sense of hope and help a student see the ways in which strong learning really matters?

King High School also has an instructional leadership cadre of two people from each interdisciplinary planning team, the principal, parents, and representatives of the site-based decision-making team. These people are building their capacity in highly motivating and culturally responsive pedagogical practice in concert with a district-level instructional leadership cadre comprising parents, community members, the assistant superintendent, and district-level curriculum representatives. Their primary goals, as reflected in the school's vision statement and school-improvement plan, are to support teaching and learning throughout the entire school so that pedagogy consistently encourages student motivation, to enhance student performance so that students experience high-quality academic success, and to help students experience their value to the community and world.

Teachers develop instructional practice by examining student work regularly. They also develop it through two-hour bimonthly interdisciplinary professional learning teams led on a rotating basis by team members. Each learning team has two members who are part of the instructional leadership cadre. Although everyone is encouraged to share resources and practices that can influence student learning, instructional cadre members routinely identify new books, materials, and demonstration sites that may be of interest. Study groups have agreed to apply their learning to collaboratively designed interdisciplinary lessons that respond to genuine student interests. In addition, teachers visit each other's classrooms every other week to observe classroom practice for thirty minutes, identify effective approaches to reaching all students, and share ideas for heightened success. Once a month, a team of teachers visits another school to engage in dialogue about school-improvement efforts and to learn from classrooms and community programs at the host school. All teachers are encouraged to present what they are learning and doing at professional conferences and school-sponsored community forums with parents, service-learning partners, business partners, and other members of the community.

Teachers refer to classroom visits that occur within their building as partnership observation and dialogue. The goals that teachers set for these visits are consistent with the goals they have identified at professional performance meetings with colleagues and school administrators. For example, one goal might be to find ways to help their lowest-performing students experience intellectual stature within the classroom. A second goal might be to share ideas on how to make the real-life experiences and values of all students a regular and highly visible part of the curriculum. Insights from partnership observation dialogue influence lesson plans that professional learning teams develop.

The two-hour block of time for professional learning teams is provided by students' participation in community service. Twice a month on Tuesday afternoons, students work in pairs or small groups to maintain a community garden and prepare meals for the community food-share program, develop a school-based day-care center with parents and community representatives, work with local visual artists on displays and maintain exhibits of student art throughout the building, create with a local video artist films about important social and community issues, share computer skills through the teaching of English as a second language at the learning center of a nearby migrant housing complex, assist in the school-based community health clinic, adopt a grandparent at the local nursing home, read to and play with children at the community homeless shelter, maintain the student-run school coffee shop, and prepare for weekly book groups that students and teachers cofacilitate in Spanish and English. Students are always welcome to develop their own projects.

Community service is an important part of the family and community involvement in the school. Parent and community volunteers coordinate the program. For this reason the community service coordination center is located in the community room, an inviting and comfortable place, with a gallery of student, staff, and parent work, as well as a washing machine and drier.

Parent and community volunteers work with students in the yearlong freshman writing program to create a community service newsletter that keeps the public informed of important outcomes and opportunities. At the end of every quarter, students display something they have created as a consequence of their community work. It might be a piece of literature, original art, or a photographic journey. Each display offers a one-page summary of the student's experience. The summaries are included in a King High School community service process-folio that parent volunteers also organize.

Parents serve many other roles as well. For example, they work with older students to coordinate an initiative that helps students who are new to the school feel respected and connected right away. Approximately one hundred older students serve as friends and advisers to small groups of new students who meet regularly throughout a student's first year at school. To further contribute to King's family atmosphere, all homeroom classes are a mix of ninth through twelfth graders. Because parent participation is essential in creating and sustaining these kinds of school-based innovations, several parents have become interested in full-time work at the school. As a consequence of receiving funding from a grant that parents and teachers applied for, five parents are assistants in training, participating in a paraprofessional training program that benefits parents and the school.

As reflected in its vision statement, King requires that students respectfully work together and engage in motivating and successful learning experiences that have personal, cultural, and community relevance. In all classrooms teachers use four questions to guide lesson development and refine learning experiences:

- How does this learning experience contribute to developing as a community of learners who feel respected and connected to one another?
- How does this learning experience offer meaningful choices and focus on personal and cultural relevance?
- How does this learning experience engage all students in challenging learning that has social merit?
- How does this learning experience support each student in knowing that he or she is becoming more effective in learning that he or she values and can use in authentic ways?

A focus group of students helped reword the four questions so that they could be clear from a student's perspective. Using these questions, students self-assess their overall performance and set goals at least once a month in every discipline. This also provides feedback to teachers on the effectiveness of classroom pedagogy. The students' questions are these:

- What have I done to demonstrate respect and support for other people in our classroom and in the community?
- What kinds of choices have I made this month that have helped me to feel some control over what I am learning?
- When was I so involved in learning that time seemed to fly?
- What are at least two things I can do to have this feeling more often, and what might my teacher do to help?
- What are some of the things I have been doing in school that allow me to feel successful?
- How are they important to other people as well as to me?

These questions help students to think deeply about their learning. They also inspire teachers to organize student learning around complex problems and issues that students care about and to support students as decision makers who are becoming their own best teachers.

To support learning, computers are integrated into all subjects. For example, a science teacher and math teacher collaborated to help students design original research on student-generated environmental questions. One such research team investigated the influence of pesticides on the health of people who live in rural communities. They designed surveys on the Internet and sent them to county health officials, medical clinics, migrant labor centers across the country, and professors at colleges and universities. (They developed a separate questionnaire to interview people in their neighborhoods.) Students used technology to compute and report their findings and to write and send an article to the local newspaper. They also developed charts and graphs for presentations to the local health board and to an environmental health class at a nearby college. Students are currently exploring ways to solve the problems they identified as a part of their research. As people who are becoming expert in some aspect of solving an environmental problem, students will eventually host an exhibit of their recommendations for their families and other community members.

The King High School governance council, which the principal, a teacher, and a parent cofacilitate, comprises teachers (including an instructional leader), parents, the assistant principal, a counselor, a district office liaison, students, and community members from several organizations. It meets once a month to assess the school's progress toward its vision, to propose solutions to complex issues that the broader school community will eventually consider, to guide the implementation of a policy to attract and retain staff members from ethnically and culturally diverse backgrounds, to garner community resources to provide support for improving the curriculum for ethnic and cultural plurality, and to serve as the school's disciplinary board. The school principal is a colearner who helps maintain a school culture that respects multiple perspectives.

King High School is proud that its students score above the national norms and that it has been recognized for the numbers of students from all backgrounds that score well above the required competency levels of state tests. However, it is understated about this because it believes that test scores are a consequence of what it most values: a stimulating place of learning with students who feel respect and support as people, students, and world citizens.

Appendix A

How Walkthroughs Open Doors

Margery B. Ginsberg and Damon Murphy

Every Thursday, the associate principal at Spring Woods High School in Houston, Texas, spends twenty minutes walking through the school's five algebra classrooms during first period. He notes each classroom's layout, the curriculum for the day, and the level of engagement among students. He speaks with one or two students in each class, asking them whether they understand the material and know where to get extra help. He notices similarities and differences among the classrooms and how teachers' strategies influence student learning.

Returning to his office, he writes some quick e-mails: "Way to go!" to a teacher who was doing a particularly great job, and a message to the math department chair about how the visits went. The e-mails are typically brief and positive, but they may also contain a question, such as, "Would you mind if I share your approach to group work with our new teachers?" or "What have you found to be successful with the students who were messing around by the window? If their behavior is typical and you'd like to share ideas, I'd enjoy putting our heads together." Sometimes he places a sticky note in a teacher's box with a "Thank you!" and a positive observation.

During a walkthrough of English classes on another day, the associate principal gets caught up in watching a dramatic presentation of portions of *King Lear* in a twelfth-grade class. In addition to performing modern-day renditions of the play, students are reciting material that they have written themselves in response to a scene that they had studied. Moving on, the associate principal visits another twelfth-grade English class that is also successfully studying *King Lear,* but in a more traditional way. That afternoon, he sends an e-mail to the more traditional teacher stating that he appreciated her well-organized presentation. He also suggests that she might enjoy sharing ideas with the teacher whose students were making presentations of the material. A week later, the principal receives a special invitation to the more traditional classroom, where he finds students performing modern-day renditions of the play.

Benefits of Walkthroughs

Administrators usually visit classrooms only when they need to conduct formal teacher evaluations. A few, however, make a practice of stopping in and walking through a few classrooms every day. These frequent, short, unscheduled visits can foster focused, reflective, and collaborative adult learning; generally, teachers welcome the opportunities for feedback and discussion that walkthroughs provide. Yet, even though staff members are more likely to accept and admire those who make time for walkthroughs, many administrators omit them from their daily schedules.

how they know what goes on?

Typically, they neglect walkthroughs because their professional preparation did not include practice in this approach. Administrators still tend to focus on visiting classrooms two or three times a year, following a protocol prescribed by state or district policy. Administrators also face urgent matters requiring their immediate attention every day, so putting off regular visits to classrooms seems justified, and they hope that visiting classes for evaluation purposes fulfills at least a minimum standard for instructional leadership. In addition, most principals do not have coaches to demonstrate the potential benefits of walkthroughs, even in schools where teachers regularly visit one another's classrooms to provide collegial support.

What are the benefits of implementing a daily schedule of short, unscheduled walkthroughs?

- Administrators become more familiar with the school's curriculum and teachers' instructional practices.

- Administrators can gauge the climate of a school: Are students engaged? Are cross-curricular concepts a part of everyday teaching? Are new teachers catching on?

- A team atmosphere develops as teachers and administrators examine instruction and student motivation and achievement together.

- Administrators establish themselves as campus leaders and instructional mentors, influencing teaching, learning, and ongoing school renewal.

- Students see that both administrators and teachers value instruction and learning.

Few administrative tools provide these benefits better than walkthroughs. Administrators report that these classroom visits also contribute to their own knowledge about teaching and learning, the essence of school renewal.

But how can administrators develop comfort and skill with this form of instructional leadership?

Getting Started

Administrators and teachers should work together to create a walkthrough protocol that makes sense from everyone's perspective, with a schedule for reviewing the process after an initial trial period. Together, teachers and administrators can determine their school's approach by asking several important questions.

- How can the walkthrough process contribute to our school's approach to renewal?

- What are some of the reasons for conducting periodic walkthroughs? Who should visit classrooms? Which rooms? How often?

- What questions should observers bring to walkthroughs? What questions should observers ask students?

- What other data can we gather and analyze to complement insights from walkthroughs?

- How can we create a positive experience for all participants?

Basic Procedures and Questions

Each school must create walkthrough procedures and a set of questions that observers should seek to answer during walkthroughs. At Spring Woods High School—a large, diverse, high-poverty, urban high school that has received national awards for its professional development and school reform—campus-based administrators are working together to set aside twenty minutes every day for visiting classrooms. This length of time might seem inconsequential, but twenty minutes a day across a five-day week, multiplied by the number of administrators in the school, computes to many hours of observation time.

A walkthrough need not be long, certainly averaging no longer than five minutes in each classroom. The key is consistency and commitment. Replacing these twenty minutes with other responsibilities is easy, but the benefits of walkthroughs far outweigh the difficulties of sticking to the schedule.

Walk the entire room. Don't get trapped at the door. A good memory device is to physically touch the back wall of each visited classroom.

The observer's questions (Hall, 2001) can include the following:

Is there a clear academic focus? Can I ascertain the purpose and expectations of the lesson when I enter the classroom—through what I see on the wall or hear from the teacher and students?

What is the level of student engagement? In general, is the movement, sound, or silence productive? Is student engagement high (80–100 percent), medium (40–79 percent), or low (0–39 percent)? What specific student behaviors indicate the level of engagement?

What do the walls of the classroom show? Is the environment pleasant and innovative? Look for displays of

- Exemplary work
- Specific scoring criteria (or specific standards and targeted benchmark skills)
- Writing samples with scoring rubrics
- Helpful information on mechanics of writing (such as capitalization and punctuation skills)
- Helpful information on problem solving
- Classroom agreements (ground rules).

How well do students understand the assignment? Select at least two students to speak to quietly and quickly, either at their desks or in the hallway. Ask them some questions:

- What are you working on?
- Why are you doing this work?
- Is what you are working on interesting to you?
- Is what you are working on in other classes interesting to you?
- What do you do in this class if you need extra help?
- Do you have a portfolio? May I see one or two examples of work from this class?

Students' answers should go beyond identifying an assignment. The goal is for students to be able to identify the skills they are working on and why. Encourage them to do their best.

Do students communicate effectively and demonstrate critical thinking skills? Do I see evidence of productive communication styles and higher-order questioning? Can students respond in ways that include personal perspectives and imaginative and thoughtful analyses of new information?

Observation Follow-up

Unless a teacher requests additional time to reflect together on walkthrough observations, administrators should keep their observation comments and feedback to the teachers simple. The administrators and staff should decide in advance on the purpose and format of the walkthrough feedback process. When discussing walkthroughs with teachers, observers may want to mention what they noticed, their questions and compliments, and possibilities for improving equitable and high-quality student learning. In general, informational and supportive feedback is more productive than evaluative comments, with additional coaches or mentors available for more extensive support.

Walkthroughs in Context

At Spring Woods High School, walkthroughs complement other forms of professional development—such as peer coaching, videotaping, and reflecting on student work—and are part of an overall framework for collaborative learning. A team of parent, teacher, and administrative representatives helps the school maintain this framework. All staff members work together to examine many kinds of data—conventional and creative (Ginsberg, 2001)—and to develop a shared language of teaching and learning, a pedagogical compass that helps the community pull in the same direction. The district staff ensures continuity between school and district goals. In other words, advocacy for constant school renewal operates at every level (Ginsberg & Wlodkowski, 2000).

Principals who are instructional leaders create, with teachers, structures that promote focused dialogue about teaching and learning. The demands of a school day, the school year, and shifting political agendas can easily interrupt this level of thoughtfulness. Nonetheless, challenging teachers and administrators to discuss the whys and hows of what they do is crucial for ongoing school renewal. In the context of a school's collaborative culture, walkthroughs provide an effective structure for this kind of dialogue.

References

Ginsberg, M. B. (2001). By the numbers. *Journal of Staff Development, 22*(2), 44–47.

Ginsberg, M. B., & Wlodkowski, R. J. (2000). *Creating highly motivating classrooms: A schoolwide approach to powerful teaching with diverse learners.* San Francisco: Jossey-Bass.

Hall, R. (2001). Unpublished walkthrough document. (Available from Bay Region IV School Support Center, Alameda County Office of Education, 313 W. Winton Ave., Hayward, CA 94544; rhall@acoe.k12.ca.us; 510–670–4170.)

Appendix B

By the Numbers

Margery B. Ginsberg

THERE ARE NO SCRIPTS for teaching in culturally diverse classrooms because culture is not an isolated part of life. As an adult educator who regularly provides demonstration classes to encourage teachers to question their practice, I know that it's nearly impossible to ever "get it right." In fact, one of the beautiful things about the education profession is that we work with human beings, none of whom can be reduced to a checklist of pedagogical or cultural terms.

A framework that helps teachers identify strengths and ideas for more equitable and motivational teaching can help them focus on the core of school renewal—everyday instructional practice.

The Motivational Framework for Culturally Responsive Teaching (Ginsberg & Wlodkowski, 2000) helps the schools with which I work focus on teaching, learning, and equity. Data-in-a-Day, an action research approach, uses the framework to help teachers take a snapshot of what teaching and learning look like in their school. By disaggregating and examining the data, staff can begin planning for improvements to eliminate differences in achievement among student groups. The framework helps take the guesswork out of how to do that, once the data have been captured.

Examining Motivations

The high-poverty schools with which I work often scrutinize conventional data: standardized tests, promotion and retention rates, attendance records,

Margery Ginsberg. "By the numbers." *Journal of Staff Development*, Spring 2001, 22(2). Reprinted with permission of National Staff Development Council, 2003. All rights reserved.

and so forth. But such data don't help teachers understand effective classroom practices or help them talk about how to create conditions that contribute to intrinsic motivation and learning among diverse student groups. Using only conventional data doesn't help address education's foremost challenge—how to support students' intrinsic motivation given the diversity of experiences, beliefs, and learning modes in today's classrooms.

Students will challenge themselves more and learn more when they value and have an interest in learning—intrinsic motivation—than when they are motivated by reward and punishment (Deci & Ryan, 1985; McCombs & Whistler, 1997).

Data-in-a-Day encourages understanding that all people have intrinsic motivations and how that motivation can be supported across all racial, ethnic, and cultural groups. The framework has four motivational conditions that apply to a range of racial, ethnic, and cultural backgrounds. When used as part of instructional design, these four conditions encourage learning.

When students can see that what they are learning makes sense and is important according to their values and perspectives, motivation emerges like a cork rising through water (Ginsberg & Wlodkowski, 2000). Data-in-a-Day can help create those environments—for teachers as well as students.

Teachers on visitation teams can visit classrooms and see clear examples of practices that engage students of varying demographic groups. Schools then can design learning experiences that honor the diverse perspectives, values, and talents that students bring to the classroom and increase students' value for and interest in learning. When educators examine student work, develop and reflect upon demonstration lessons, review videotapes of classroom interactions, or initiate peer coaching, they

---

Motivational Framework

Data-in-a-Day teams focus on four conditions that form the motivational framework—how classroom practices:

- Help students respect and feel connected to each other and to their teachers (inclusion)

- Help students develop a positive attitude toward learning by offering a relevant curriculum (positive attitude)

- Create learning experiences that challenge and engage diverse students (meaning)

- Assess what matters to students and society (competence)

design their approach with questions based on the framework's four conditions.

Generally, teachers and other members of the school community base their impressions of classroom practices on what they hear or talk about with a few teachers. By applying the Data-in-a-Day process and the Motivational Framework, staff have a truer picture of everyday practices and can begin to talk about the distance between pedagogical ideals and everyday practices. This can lead to a more cohesive school improvement plan and focused professional development.

Organizing Data-in-a-Day

Generally, Data-in-a-Day is a three-day self-study. It can be adapted according to a school's logistical challenges. This outline is based on the most effective approaches for groups with whom I have worked.

The first step is establishing a planning committee of about five teacher-leaders from the school, two parents, and, at the high school level, at least two students, as well as building and district-level administrators (see Exhibit B.1). This committee is needed to communicate with the rest of the school, organize a team preparation dinner, and produce a brief video of a teaching segment to prepare teams to identify motivational attributes and to use the framework. Committee members also are guides and leaders for classroom visitation teams, develop visitation schedules, and participate in all team activities. Having a coordinator to ensure that the planning team has maximum support for each task is essential.

After the planning committee is selected, it drafts a brief letter to the faculty explaining the what, why, how, who, and when of the process. (See Exhibit B.2.) At this time, the committee asks for a teacher volunteer who will be videotaped to help visitation teams apply the rubric based on the Motivational Framework. As an alternative, a professionally prepared tape, such as *Good Morning, Miss Toliver*, can be used. As team members watch the demonstration video, they practice looking for the motivational condition for which they will be responsible during classroom visits.

The Data-in-a-Day process begins with an evening dinner to develop a sense of community and prepare teams. Throughout the next day, all of the teams visit classrooms and collect data. The teams discuss their observations with five items in mind:

- Examples of how teachers address the framework's four conditions

- Motivational conditions with which teachers are most comfortable or show competence in

- Any aspects of motivating teaching that were not apparent at the time of the visits
- Wishes or suggestions that might assist teachers
- Insights students offer

At the end of the third day, generally just after school, Data-in-a-Day teams share insights with faculty. Insights can spark dialogue, generate additional inquiry, enhance individual and schoolwide goals, and focus professional development activities.

Some schools, especially the first time they initiate Data-in-a-Day, prefer simply to list examples of highly motivating practices and then to note questions the school could ask itself based on these observations. For example, after observing mostly teacher-directed instruction, one team posed this question: How might we more actively involve students in learning?

In another school, teams consistently reported that the fourth motivational condition, engendering competence, wasn't seen. The group talked about assessment and grading practices, a conversation that led teachers to use team planning time to share and design more motivationally effective approaches to assessment and grading. And the school as a whole began to talk about varying philosophies on grading and research on the limited or negative impact of grades on the performance of low- and middle-performing students (Stiggins, 1988; Wlodkowski & Ginsberg, 1995).

Learning from Data-in-a-Day

Evaluations of Data-in-a-Day have been positive. Comments included, "We were of varied backgrounds, but we often observed or shared similar feelings." Participants said the benefits were: "hearing students' points of view," "seeing different subjects and different approaches," "listening to the perspectives of students and parents," and "help(ing) my school make itself better."

Some common challenges noted were: "Some students seemed to be nonparticipants and were even excluded from the classroom community"; "It seems like the school as a whole might need more help working with groups"; "It looks like we still have many classrooms in which the teacher is dispensing information to a relatively passive class." Although students on visitation teams typically shared these perspectives, they also realized the effect of classroom behavior, as in the comment, "I never understood before how hard it is for the teacher when I talk so much to my friends in class."

Data-in-a-Day promotes attributes that successful schools share: engaging students, parents, community members, and district-level personnel in continuous renewal; job-embedded learning with a clear focus on teaching and learning; and, in districts such as Spring Branch, Texas, Fremont, California, and Richmond, California, questioning assumptions about how effort and reward are driving forces in academic achievement among diverse learners.

Participants frequently comment that Data-in-a-Day would be an excellent precursor to schoolwide peer coaching.

Conclusion

More and more, states are requiring school districts to look at test scores according to race, poverty, and gender so that schools will acknowledge and deal with differences in achievement. Educators may be sensitive to this requirement because schools often are caught in shifting or superficial political agendas. Yet individual schools can be inspiring examples of how looking at data and acting on it can contribute to reversing the academic effects of racism and poverty.

References

Deci, E. L., & Ryan, E. M. (1985). *Intrinsic motivation and self-determination in human behavior.* New York: Plenum.

Ginsberg, M. B., & Wlodkowski, R. J. (2000). *Creating highly motivating classrooms for all students: A schoolwide approach to powerful teaching with diverse learners.* San Francisco: Jossey-Bass.

McCombs, B. L., & Whistler, J. S. (1997). *The learner-centered classroom and school: Strategies for increasing student motivation and achievement.* San Francisco: Jossey-Bass.

Stiggins, R. J. (1998). Revitalizing classroom assessment: The highest instructional priority. *Phi Delta Kappan,* January, pp. 363–368.

Wlodkowski, R. J., & Ginsberg, M. B. (1995) *Diversity and motivation: Culturally responsive teaching.* San Francisco: Jossey-Bass.

EXHIBIT B.1

Building the Team

Team Composition

Ideally, teams should represent the demographic makeup of the school, including parents as well as teachers and administrators, and, at the middle and high school level, students. Student representation is especially important and should include low-, middle-, and high-performing students. Tenth and eleventh grade participants are particularly valuable because they are familiar with high school, and since they are not graduating in the near future, they can sustain their relationships with team members. In fact, in some cases, participation in this process has been the first step to establishing mentorships between student and adult participants.

A Few Suggestions

1. Be very clear about the purpose and how data will look and be used.
2. Recruit more than enough volunteers for teams to guarantee enough members in case of sickness.
3. Recruit volunteers and schedule classrooms to be visited well in advance.
4. Provide a comfortable place for visitation teams to refresh themselves.
5. Put the debriefing process in writing.
6. Establish clear agreements with faculty about how to maintain an environment in which student participants feel safe enough to express their perspectives.
7. Repeat the process until all faculty have participated in visitations.
8. Make certificates of appreciation for all participants, accompanied, if possible, by a photograph of the visit.

Team Preparation Sample Agenda

Time	Topic	Facilitator
5:30–6:00	Dinner	
6:00–6:05	Introduction	Principal and coordinator
6:05–6:15	Personal introductions	Teams
6:15–6:45	Introduction to the motivational framework	External consultant, principal, or coach
6:45–7:00	Recording information and using the motivational framework	Same as above
7:00–7:20	Video	External consultant or coach
7:20–7:40	Discussion	Expert groups (representatives from different teams who share the same motivational condition)
7:40–7:50	Visitation protocols and helpful hints	Designated member of the planning committee
7:50–7:55	Logistics	Coordinator
7:55–8:15	Questions, comments	Coordinator

EXHIBIT B.2

Sample Initial Communication

What? Data-in-a-Day

This event provides an opportunity for stakeholders to observe educational practice in our school and to collect information we can use to understand the ways in which we are supporting student motivation and meeting some of the challenges we still face.

Why? Is This Really Important?

We are committed to highly motivating teaching and learning and have been finding ways to strengthen classroom practice in support of the diverse students we serve. However, none of our data provide perspective on how we look on any given day—and what we can do to provide ongoing support to each other, given the range of expertise in our school. Data will be used to share successes and engage the school community in dialogue about how we might tackle challenging areas of classroom practice. None of the data will contain teachers' names (unless teachers would like to reveal that themselves). As a school with many accomplishments, we may not easily see the gaps that exist between what we say we are doing and what we are really doing. Data-in-a-Day can enhance our commitment to always seeing ourselves as "in progress."

How? Teams, Visitation Rubrics, Visitation Protocols

There will be eight teams of five people (two students, one parent, one teacher, and a team leader) to accurately reflect our demographics. Each team will visit six different classrooms during first, second, and third periods for thirty minutes. By the end of the day, teams will have collectively visited forty-eight classrooms. Each team member will use an observation tool that concentrates on one condition of the motivational framework (inclusion, positive attitude, meaning, or competence). They will look for ways in which classroom practice demonstrates the presence of the condition. At the conclusion of the six classroom visits, team members will meet and share their observations with other Data-in-a-Day team members who looked for the same motivational condition. For example, all of the people who looked for inclusion will meet and compare notes. After they compare results, look for trends, identify areas of strength, and areas that seem to need support to increase student success, they will develop a way to share information with the whole faculty. This information will be shared at the end of the school day that follows the classroom visitation day.

Who?

We need teachers to volunteer to be on Data-in-a-Day teams, and we also need teachers to suggest student volunteers, parent volunteers, and to volunteer their classrooms for a visit. Even if these classrooms tend to reflect "best practices," it will give the school an understanding of what "best practices" look like right now. Please contact (name of coordinator) by (date). Because teachers are often modest about their teaching or cautious about being visited while working with students, we will probably need to invite people to volunteer and hope that you will consider this. This process will provide a valuable service to all of us—and especially our students. A tribute to participating teachers will precede our sessions with faculty as a whole.

Where Can I Get More Information?

(List names of organizing committee). Thank you!

Motivational Framework Guide

Margery B. Ginsberg

Establishing Inclusion

How does the learning experience contribute to the development of students as a community of learners who feel respected *by and connected to* one another and to the teacher?

Routines and rituals are visible and understood by all.

- Rituals are in place that help students feel that they belong in the class.

- Students have opportunities to learn about each other.

- Students and teacher have opportunities to learn about each other's unique backgrounds.

- Class agreements or participation guidelines and consequences for violating agreements are negotiated.

- The system of personal and collective responsibility for agreements is understood by everyone and applied with fairness.

All students equitably and actively participate and interact.

- The teacher directs attention equitably.

- The teacher interacts respectfully with all students.

- The teacher demonstrates to all students that she or he cares about them.

- Students share ideas and perspectives with partners and small groups.

- Students respond to lessons by writing.

- Students know what to do, especially when making choices.

- Students help each other.

- Work is displayed (with students' permission).

Inclusion Activities from
Creating Highly Motivating Classrooms for All Students

Activity	Page
Venn Diagram Sharing	53
Two Wishes and a Truth	54
Decades and Diversity	55
Think-Pair-Share Exercises	56
"Ask Me About …" Posters	57
Multicultural Inventory	58
Bio-Poems	59
Interpretive Community Maps	60
Dialogue Journals	61
Response Cards	61
Fist-to-Five	62
Class Historian	63
Class Review	64
Bean Experiment	64
Class Agreement or Participation Guidelines	65
Note Cues	68
Cooperative Groups	68
Negotiating Conflict	72–74

Developing a Positive Attitude

How does the learning experience offer meaningful choices *and promote personal* relevance *to contribute to students' positive attitude?*

The teacher works with students to personalize the relevance of the course content.

- Students' experiences, concerns, and interests are used to develop course content.

- Students' experiences, concerns, and interests are addressed in responses to questions.

- Students' prior knowledge and their learning experiences are explicitly linked to course content and questions.

- The teacher encourages students to understand, develop, and express different points of view.

- The teacher encourages students to clarify their interests and set goals.

Attitude Activities from
Creating Highly Motivating Classrooms for All Students

Activity	Page
Carousel Graffiti	84
Scaffolding for Success	89
Scaffolding Minilectures with Human Highlighters	90
Finding Numbers	96
Reframing	101
Story Posters	108
KWL process	82–84

- The teacher maintains flexibility in the pursuit of *teachable moments* and emerging interests.

The teacher encourages students to make real choices.

- The teacher directs attention equitably.
- Students choose how to learn (multiple intelligences).
- Students choose what to learn.
- Students choose where to learn.
- Students choose when a learning experience will be considered complete.
- Students choose how learning will be assessed.
- Students choose with whom to learn.
- Students choose how to solve emerging problems.

Enhancing Meaning

How does the learning experience engage *all students in* challenging *learning that has social merit?*

The teacher encourages all students to learn, create, and communicate knowledge.

- The teacher helps students to activate prior knowledge and to use it as a guide to learning.
- The teacher, in concert with students, creates opportunities for inquiry, investigation, and projects.
- The teacher provides opportunities for students to actively participate in challenging ways when not involved in sedentary activities, such as reflecting, reading, and writing.

Meaning Activities from
Creating Highly Motivating Classrooms for All Students

Activity	Page
Where I'm From	134
Fishbowl Questioning Procedure	138
Guided Reciprocal Questioning	140
Learning Activities That Stimulate Critical Thinking	144
Case Study	146

- The teacher asks higher order questions of all students throughout a lesson.
- The teacher uses multiple *safety nets* to ensure student success (for example, not grading all assignments, asking students to work with partners, designing cooperative learning experiences).

Engendering Competence

How does the learning experience create students' understanding that they are becoming more effective in authentic learning that they value?

There is information, consequence, or product that supports students in valuing and identifying learning.

- The teacher clearly communicates the purpose of the lesson.
- The teacher clearly communicates criteria for excellent final products.
- The teacher provides opportunities for a diversity of competencies to be demonstrated in a variety of ways.
- The teacher helps all students to concretely identify accomplishments.
- The teacher assesses different students differently.
- The teacher assesses progress continually in order to provide feedback on individual growth and progress.
- The teacher creates opportunities for students to make explicit connections between new and prior learning.
- The teacher creates opportunities for students to make explicit connections between their learning and the real world.
- The teacher provides opportunities for students to self-assess learning in order to reflect on their growth as learners.
- The teacher provides opportunities for students to self-assess their personal responsibility for contributing to the classroom as a learning community.

Competence Activities from
Creating Highly Motivating Classrooms for All Students

References

Allen, L., Rogers, D. Hensley, F., Gladon, M., Livingston, M. *A Guide to Renewing Your School: Lessons from the League of Professional Schools.* San Francisco: Jossey-Bass, 1999.

Bernhardt, V. L. *The School Portfolio: A Comprehensive Framework for School Improvement.* (2nd ed.) Larchmont, N.Y.: Eye in Education, 1999.

Champion, R. H. *Tools for Change.* Ellicot City, Md.: National Staff Development Council, 1993.

Cohen, D. K., McLaughlin, M. W., and Talbert, J. E. (eds.) *Teaching for Understanding: Challenges for Policy and Practice.* San Francisco: Jossey-Bass, 1993.

Darling-Hammond, L., and McLaughlin, M. W. "Policies that Support Professional Development in an Era of Reform." *Phi Delta Kappan,* 1995, 76(8), 597–604.

Deci, E. L., and Ryan, R. M. *Intrinsic Motivation and Self-Descrimination in Human Behavior.* New York: Plenum, 1985.

Deci, E. L., and Ryan, R. M. "A Motivational Approach to Self: Integration in Personality." In R. Dienstbier (ed.), *Nebraska Symposium on Motivation,* Vol. 38, Lincoln: University of Nebraska Press, 1991.

DuFour, R. "One Clear Voice is Needed in the Din." *Journal of Staff Development,* 2002, 23(2), 60–61.

Easton, L. B. *Powerful Designs for Professional Development.* Oxford, Ohio: National Staff Development Council, 2003.

Elmore, R. F. "The Limits of Change." *Harvard Education Letter,* January/February 2002.

Fordham, S., and Ogbu, J. "Black Students' School Success: Coping with the Burden of 'Acting White.'" *Urban Review,* 1986, *18,* 176–206.

Francis, S., Hirsh, S., and Rowland, E. "Improving School Culture through Study Groups." *Journal of Staff Development*, 1994, *15*(2), 12–15.

Fullan, M G., and Miles, M. B. "Getting Reform Right: What Works and What Doesn't." *Phi Delta Kappan*, 1992, *73*(10), 745–752.

Gay, G. *Culturally Responsive Teaching: Theory, Research, and Practice.* New York: Teachers College Press, 2000.

Ginsberg, M. B. "By the Numbers." *Journal of Staff Development*, 2001, *22*(2), 44–47.

Ginsberg, M. B., and Johnson, J. F. "Beyond Fixing Kids: School Support Teams Offer Innovative Support for Strengthening High Poverty Schools." *Journal of Staff Development*, 1998, *19*(2), 23–27.

Ginsberg, M. B., Johnson, J. F., and Moffett, C. A. *Educators Supporting Educators: A Guide to Organizing School Support Teams.* Alexandria, Va.: Association for Supervision and Curriculum Development, 1997.

Ginsberg, M. B., and Murphy, D. "How Walk-throughs Open Doors." *Educational Leadership*, 2002, *59*(8), 34–36.

Ginsberg, M. B., and Wlodkowski, R. J. *Creating Highly Motivating Classrooms for All Students: A Schoolwide Approach to Powerful Teaching with Diverse Learners.* San Francisco: Jossey-Bass, 2000.

Good Morning Miss Toliver. Los Angeles, Calif.: Foundation for Advancement in Science and Education, 1993. Video. http://www.fasenet.org/store/kay_toliver/gmmt.html

Hilliard, A. G. "Teachers and Cultural Styles in a Pluralistic Society," *NEA Today,* 1989, *7*(6), 65–69.

Hirsh, S. (Ed.). *School Team Innovator.* Oxford, Ohio: National Staff Development Council, n.d.

Hirsh, S., Delehant, A., and Sparks, S. *Keys to Successful Meetings.* Oxford, Ohio: National Staff Development Council, 1994.

Irvine, J .J., and York, D. E. "Learning Styles and Culturally Diverse Students: A Literature Review." In J. A. Banks and C.A.M. Banks (eds.), *Handbook of Research on Multicultural Education* (pp. 484–497). New York: Macmillan, 1995.

King, J. "Thank You for Opening Our Minds: On Praxis, Transmutation, and Black Studies in Teacher Development." In J. King, E. Hollins, and W. Hayman (eds.), *Preparing Teachers for Cultural Diversity.* New York: Teachers College Press, 1997.

Kitayama, S., and Markus, H. R. (eds.). *Emotion and Culture: Empirical Studies of Mutual Influence.* Washington, D.C.: American Psychological Association, 1994.

Ladson-Billings, G. *The Dream Keepers: Successful Teachers of African American Children.* San Francisco: Jossey-Bass, 1994.

Ladson-Billings, G. (with Mary Louise Gomez). "Just Showing Up: Supporting Early Literacy Through Teachers' Professional Communities." *Phi Delta Kappan,* 2001, *82*(9), 675–680.

Lambert, N. M., and McCombs, B. L. "Introduction: Learner Centered Schools and Classrooms as a Direction for School Reform." In N. M. Lambert and B. L. McCombs (eds.), *How Students Learn: Reforming Schools Through Learner-Centered Education.* Washington, D.C.: American Psychological Association, 1998.

Lewis, A. C. "Responding Wisely to the Bush Plan." *Phi Delta Kappan,* March 2001, 488.

McCombs, B. L., and Whistler, J. S. *The Learner-Centered Classroom and School: Strategies for Increasing Student Motivation and Achievement.* San Francisco: Jossey-Bass, 1997.

Murphy, C. "Finding Time for Faculties to Study Together." *Journal of Staff Development,* 1997, *18*(3).

Newmann, F. "Linking Restructuring to Authentic Student Achievement." *Phi Delta Kappan,* 1991, 72(6), 458–463.

Nieto, S. *Affirming Diversity.* White Plains, N.Y.: Longman Publishing Group, 1992.

Noguera, P. A., and Moran Brown, E. (2002) www.boston globe.com/daily-globe2/263/oped/Educating_America_s_new_majoirty+.shtml

Ogle, D. "The K-W-L: A Teaching Model That Develops Active Reading of Expository Text." *The Reading Teacher,* 1986, *39*, 564–576.

Ovando, C. J., and Collier, V. P. *Bilingual and ESL Classrooms.* New York: McGraw-Hill, 1985.

Raywid, M. A. "Finding Time for Collaboration." *Educational Leadership,* September 1993.

Rothwell, W. J., and Kazanas, H. C. *Mastering the Instructional Design Process: A Systematic Approach.* San Francisco: Jossey-Bass, 1992.

Schlechty, P. *Inventing Better Schools.* San Francisco: Jossey-Bass, 1997.

Shade, B. J., Kelly, C., and Oberg, M. *Creating Culturally Responsive Classrooms.* Washington, D.C.: American Psychological Association, 1997.

Stiggins, R. *Student Involved Classroom Assessment.* Englewood Cliffs, N.J.: Prentice Hall, 2001.

Tatum, B. D. *"Why are All the Black Kids Sitting Together in the Cafeteria?" and Other Conversations About Race.* New York: Basic Books, 1997.

Villa, R. A., and Thousand, J. S. *Creating an Inclusive School.* Alexandria, Va.: Association for Supervision and Curriculum Development, 1995.

Wlodkowski, R. J. *Enhancing Adult Motivation to Learn.* (2nd ed.) San Francisco: Jossey-Bass, 2000.

Wlodkowski, R. J., and Ginsberg, M. B. *Diversity and Motivation: Culturally Responsive Teaching.* San Francisco: Jossey-Bass, 1995 (paperback edition, 2003)

Index